WILL BITCOINS TAKE

OVER THE US DOLLAR?

WHAT HAPPENS WHEN ALL BITCOINS

ARE MINED

Talluah Dandress

TABLE OF CONTENT

Introduction

First I'm going to explain exactly why the decline of the US Dollar is one of the most bullish signals yet for the long-term prospects of Bitcoin. Next, you will learn what happens when all the Bitcoin is mined, will the Bitcoin network grind to a halt and bring the entire cryptocurrency space crashing down with it, how long do we have before this happens and what solutions we have for this problem. Moving on, I'm going to go over the safest crypto wallets that money can buy and I'm also going to share a few essential crypto tips when it comes to using these devices. After that, I'll be sharing my complete beginner's guide on how to buy cryptocurrency safely. I'll be taking you through all the steps without any of that technical jargon, so you can buy crypto the right way and store those coins securely. Next, I'm going to explain how Ethereum gas works, how you can reduce gas fees and how you can even profit from these rising gas costs. After that, we will cover decentralized identity management and how to use lending protocols for crypto loans using Litentry. Next, you will learn about centralized DeFi ecosystems such as Kusama and ThorChain to see if there is more to these projects. Next, I will be comparing Cardano and Polkadot and reveal which one has the best chance of becoming the next Ethereum for smart contracts and decentralized cryptocurrency applications. Lastly, I'm going to be taking a closer look at the Binance coin, the Huobi token and the FTX token to understand what's the future holds for their potential price action. Finally, I'll explain exactly how to buy Bitcoin with that regular fiat currency on Binance, I'll walk also you through how to trade on the exchange various ways and I'll provide you with a complete overview of Binance's other major features that you can capitalize in a long run.

Chapter 1 - Will Bitcoin takes over the US Dollar?

For years, the US Dollar has reigned as the World's most widely used and widely held currency. The monetary equivalent of a global heart that keeps the blood of trade flowing. However, more recently this status has begun to wane. Some say that this could be the beginning of a trend that sees other currencies and assets taking its place. Bad news? Well, that all depends on who you are and what you own. In this chapter I'm going to tell you exactly why the decline of the US Dollar is one of the most bullish signals yet for the long-term prospects of Bitcoin. So, if you hold Bitcoin or are thinking of investing in it, then you cannot afford to miss what I'm about to share with you. The Dollar is an asset and its value is of course determined by its price. So how has that price been doing recently? Well, not too good. The best way to get a sense of the value of a currency is to compare it to that of its global trading partners. This is why we have the US Dollar index. The US Dollar index is it's just a measure of the exchange rate of USD to a basket of currencies of the US's global trading partners. This index has been on a sustained decline since the beginning of 2020. In effect it is down by over 10 percent since the beginning of March 2020. What was driving this? Well, it comes down to one of the most fundamental economic disciplines of all; supply and demand. Like Newton's law of gravity, these economic principles apply to everything including the World's reserve currency. As we know from economics, the balance between the supply and demand of an asset impacts on the price of the asset. In the case of a currency, it's the price of said currency in relation to others, hence the Dollar index.

What is known from this then is that there has been an overflow of Dollars on the open marketplace with a demand that has not been capable to keep up with it. When viewed in that framework, it makes sense as to why the Dollar index is on the degeneration. There has been a rapid decline in US economic activity from the pandemic. This has meant that the natural utility demand for Dollars has been on the decline too. Nonetheless, in order to respond to the falling economic activity, the FED has turned on those printing presses. Bond buying programs and quantitative easing have meant that we have had unprecedented levels of monetary stimulus that has flooded the system with Dollars. More Dollars floating around with less demand, therefore means that the price will of course react. This is what has been driving that decline in the Dollar index there. What is important to note here though, is that this US Dollar index is a separate concept to inflation, although they are quite related. Inflation is just a comparison of the purchasing power of US Dollars to general goods and services, whereas the USD index is a comparison to other currencies. A Dollar that's weak compared to other currencies will make imports more expensive, which could of course also drive inflation. What's most important to note here, is that those people who have kept hold of US Dollars in their bank accounts have held a rapidly depreciating asset. The most important question that we need to ask ourselves is whether this is likely to continue. Well, there are a number of global macroeconomic factors that we have to look at. Factors that impact not only on the supply and demand of USD, but also this relative to other currencies. So let's start on one of the biggest and longest running drags on the currency and that is the widening trade deficit. Quite simply, the trade deficit is the difference between a country's exports and imports. Some countries may run a deficit while others have a surplus when it comes to the United States, they run a pretty large deficit of close to 540 billion Dollars. This has worsened even more since the beginning of the Covid virus, as the US opened its economy and consumers started importing goods and services. The deterioration in the current account in the second quarter of last year was the worst on record. Now the US runs a deficit with a number of countries but perhaps the biggest deficits that it runs are with China, Japan and Germany. So why is a trade deficit bad for the US Dollar? Well, if people in the US are trade in more goods and services from overseas, then they are going to be paying for this in USD. This means that those countries that are exporting to these customers will have to convert that USD into their native currency to meet their costs. This therefore means that you have a lot of selling pressure on Dollars, which of course drives down the price. That's where we are right now, but is this likely to continue? Well, I happen to think so. This is just part of the trend in the decline of US manufacturing. China has now become the main manufacturing hub in the World, which means that the US will still have to import from them. Moreover, if the numerous tariffs and barriers that Trump put up against China could not reverse the trend, then it's hard to see how Biden could top that. The only thing that could possibly slow this could be for the US to become more competitive when it comes to manufacturing. But structurally changing the US labor market is not something that can happen in a year or two, and this is just the goods component of the balance of payments deficit. You should also consider the capital component. Given that there's been an explosion in government spending and a lack of domestic saving, the US has to import surplus savings from abroad if it wants to invest and grow. The United States budget deficit is now so steep that it will be hard for them to save domestically anytime in a little while. They must import those savings and reserves. It doesn't look like things are going to be improving on the balance of payment side for quite some time. But there is another far more consequential factor that has been driving Dollar depreciation recently and that is its general oversupply. The amount of money that's been pumped into the system is truly astounding. Last year a fifth of all US money supply was printed in a single year. In its entire 107 year history, 20% of all the money in circulation was printed in 2020. I don't need to tell you what effect this has on the value of the US Dollar. Oversupply with limited demand of course decreases its value. This is not only for purchasing power and inflation, but also its value relative to other currencies; depreciation. We know that the FED has had a hand in decreasing the value of the Dollar, but is this likely to continue? Well, it seems like it may, at least for the near term. In a latest virtual summit, Powell said that monetary stimulus will remain in place well into the recovery. Given that the recovery seems to have stalled more recently, one can therefore assume that the printing presses won't be slowed anytime soon. Currently, the FED is buying 120 billion Dollars of treasuries and mortgage-backed securities every month. 120 billion Dllars of extra funds that are likely to continue for the next few months. What all this means therefore is an increasing oversupply of the US Dollar and hence a fall in its value relative to other moneys. That will be the inevitable inflation that we could face once we emerge from the pandemic. This surge of jumbo jet money is going to be a strong headwind for the US Dollar in the coming months. Nonetheless there is one more reason that could have a further drag on its value and that is its global use. More specifically, its use in trade and as a reserve currency. Ever since the inception of the Bretton Woods system back in 1944, the US Dollar has been viewed as the global reserve currency. In fact, up until 1971, all other currencies were pegged to the Dollar at a fixed rate. Yet, things have changed considerably since then. As other states have sought to limit their reliance on the USD, so too has its global use waned. This has been triggered by the pandemic and more hostile trade practices. For example, in October 2020, the Euro exceeded the Dollar as the most used currency for global payments. Something that has not happened for years, and it seems as if this trend is likely to continue. That's because the EU is now making a concerted effort to steer most European settlements towards the Euro. More recently, the European Commission has outlined plans to increase the role of the Euro in international payments and investments. For example, they're going to be offering incentives for European market participants to work with currency clearing houses that are based in Europe, and the Europeans are not alone in this. Both China and Russia have indicated that they would like to move away from their dependence on US Dollar settlement, and this was even before the pandemic and tumultuous geopolitics of the past year. What all this shows US is that demand to use greenbacks as a means to grease the wheels of global finance and trade, is likely to diminish over the coming years. As this transactional demand starts to wane so will its price relative to other currencies. This is just the use of Dollars as a medium of exchange. We should also not forget that Dollars are held by foreign central banks as a buffer to protect themselves. You can think of this as the investment demand for US Dollars. Here is a graph that shows US the US Dollar percentage of global reserve currencies.

As you can see, there's been a sustained fall in this share over the past seven years. Much of this comes down to those same geopolitical concerns that I just mentioned, but apart from that, it just makes practical sense. Why would a foreign central bank want to hold a currency, where the value of said currency can be easily impacted by the actions of the FED? Moreover, these central banks are banking on the continued solvency and strength of the US fiscals, both of which can sometimes be considered dubious. Furthermore, times have changed quite considerably for some of the largest central banks. Gone are the days when there were no reasonable alternatives to the US Dollar. Other global currencies such as the Yen, Euro and Sterling have gained market share and take a look at the growth of Chinese RMB use. That's a pretty substantial increase which came on the heels of RMB becoming an official reserve currency in 2016. It's not only been currency that these banks have been diversifying into; they've also been net buyers of gold ever since 2010. What all this means is that there's less central bank demand out there for US Dollars. Less demand to use it as a store of value. If we couple this with all of the other factors that I mentioned above, it's no surprise that the value of US Dollars has been on the decline. That's my prediction for the trajectory of the US Dollar. But fear not because I'm going to tell you why this decline in the US Dollar is the single most bullish factor that could supercharge Bitcoin. It's no longer a pipe dream. Bitcoin is emerging as one of the best bets against the declining value of the US Dollar. This is thanks to the many characteristics that make it such an amazing store of value. Limited supply, immutability and transparency. It's actually emerged as a theme among these investors. Bitcoin is an inflation and Dollar hedge that can be used to protect your wealth from these sustained trends. Firms on Wall Street are making the distinct connection between Dollar weakness, inflation and Bitcoin. These include the likes of JP Morgan, Paul Tudor Jones, Blackrock and the list goes on. You only need to take a look at the immense amount of institutional adoption that we've seen over the past year. I know what you're thinking; these are high alpha driven risk-taking Wall Streeters - of course they're comfortable with Bitcoin. Well, last year it was also announced that MassMutual an insurance fund was picking up Bitcoin. Insurance funds are much more risk-averse than your traditional money manager, and much more recently, it was disclosed that the endowments of Harvard, Yale, Brown and the University of Michigan have started buying Bitcoin. Now take a second to think about that; funds that are tasked with preserving capital for generations are investing in Bitcoin. They are a completely different investor class that's focused on steady growth and capital preservation. They're mostly global macro focused and are investing in Bitcoin based on global trends, one of which is of course hedging US Dollar devaluation. If you have Ivy League UNI Endowment funds investing in Bitcoin, how long do you think before pension funds start dipping their toes. Their investment profile is not that far removed, and Wall Street has already started building the infrastructure required in order to service these large investors needs. Take a look at all the banks and asset managers that are starting to offer Bitcoin custody solutions. Blackrock, Fidelity and even Goldman Sachs. Or, how about regulated investment funds? We all know about the explosive growth in AUM at Greyscale, but there are a number of other funds that have opened their doors. Let's also not forget that there's a raft of Bitcoin ETF applications that have been filed. We also have a more crypto friendly SEC and if one of these is approved, it will give a whole swathe of new investors an opportunity to buy into Bitcoin. This is all known and of course extremely positive for Bitcoin. But there is one investor class that could have an interest in buying some of that digital gold and it's one that I've just alluded to. There is a fairly decent chance that we could see a foreign central bank start allocating some of its reserves towards Bitcoin. It's only logical. It's a strong Dollar and inflation hedge and would allow them to diversify, away from the concept of foreign currency fiat reserves entirely. These central banks are more than willing to invest in gold as a store of value. However the latter beats the former. When it comes to a central bank, the main benefits of Bitcoin come with its ease of storage and conversion. There's no need to rely on a bank to hold cash or a vault to hold gold. A simple hardware device could theoretically hold the keys to the reserves of an entire central bank. It's not just me that thinks that central banks could dip their toes in these waters. The guys over at Masari mentioned it as a possibility in their 2021 crypto investment thesis. They see it as potentially appealing to central banks of those smaller EM currencies that are quite volatile. Still think it's a pipe dream? Well here is the ex-prime minister of Canada; actually referring to Bitcoin as an alternative reserve currency to the US Dollar.

The amount of Dollars currently held in reserves by these foreign central banks is immense. A tiny bit of diversification with a few of these banks could skyrocket the price of Bitcoin. That's just because there is very little of it to go around. It's quite clear that the value of the US Dollar is on the decline. While this trend may have been present before the pandemic, there's no doubt that it has triggered it. Furthermore, given many of the macroeconomic factors mentioned earlier, it looks like this trend is likely to continue at least for the foreseeable future. The current account deficit is growing. The FED is still printing. Foreign governments are diversifying and central banks are hedging. When combined these forces, don't seem to paint a pretty picture for USD. Of course, one man's pain is another man's gain. Dollar hedges are likely to become extremely popular. This is especially the case when devaluation is combined with broader inflation. Bitcoin is perhaps one of the best Dollar hedges out there, and that is not an opinion; it's becoming common knowledge. You only need to take a look at all the institutions, corporates funds and endowments who have allocated parts of their portfolio to Bitcoin. The last piece of that puzzle may in fact be central banks. As we've witnessed with the corporates all you need is one of them to break the stereotype, to take the plunge and hopefully start a trend. If that trend does take hold, then grab and hold of your sets because this is going to be one crazy ride. That's my miserable overview of the Dollar but super bullish view of Bitcoin.

Chapter 2 - How to buy Crypto Safely

Are you looking to dip your toes into those cryptocurrency markets and buy your first crypto? In this chapter I'll be sharing my complete beginner's guide on how to buy cryptocurrency safely. I'll be taking you through all the steps without any of that technical mumbo jumbo. All that is so you can buy crypto the right way and store those coins securely. Before I kick things off there are some cold hard crypto truths I need to share with you. Things you need to know before actually buying that crypto. Recently we have had the mainstream media going crazy over Bitcoin. Running headline after headline of Bitcoin breaking all-time highs. Not only that, but they also regularly publish mind-blowing price predictions like from JP Morgan. With that sort of coverage you could be forgiven for thinking that you can sit back relax take a bath buy crypto and just see those mad gains roll in. Well, crypto can sometimes be a bit like the wild west with hackers, scams and questionable exchanges everywhere. So if you're wanting to enter these crypto markets, then you better have your six shooter ready and be prepared to fight off those bandits. Also, if you hold cryptocurrency in a safe way, you will effectively be in possession of your own Swiss bank account, however where crypto differs is that there are no such things as transaction reversals. There is no one to really ring up if things go wrong. There's no insurance on this mini Swiss bank account and that means if your cryptocurrency is stolen, the government won't reimburse you for that loss. Another thing I've observed my friends doing, is bragging about how much money they've made in these crypto markets. I know how seeing your money double in days can be exhilarating, however who else is overhearing that conversation? There are bad people out there and they might have overheard that you hold tens of thousands of Dollars in crypto and that is just asking for trouble. So, if you're thinking about getting into crypto then I would recommend that you keep it to yourself. Seriously, the fewer people that know you hold crypto, the better. My next pearl of wisdom is that you should not invest more than you're willing to lose. Nothing is guaranteed in life and the same is true of crypto. If you're thinking about maxing out that credit card or using that rent money to buy crypto, then please don't. I also need to tell you that crypto is way more volatile than the stock market. If the stock market falls seven percent, it triggers a circuit breaker and trading stops for a bit. Hitting a seven percent loss is almost guaranteed to make the news headlines, however in crypto, that's just another day at the office. I've lived through days where my entire portfolio swung up or down by over 30 percent. If that's too much for you to handle, then crypto isn't for you. I can tell you first hand that those swings lead to a lot of stress. Another tip I need to share with you is to be careful which websites you visit. There are an overabundance of scam websites out there pretending to be crypto exchanges and wallets. Those fake websites are there to get your login and passwords and enable the crypto thief to make off with your crypto like a bandit, so make sure you pay attention to the exact URL of that crypto site and make sure you see the little padlock at the top left corner of the URL. See that and you know the site has an SSL certificate which means your password submission should be secure. Once you're sure you're on that genuine crypto website you need, it's a good idea to bookmark it and use that bookmark to access it in the future. Finally, a really important thing that confuses crypto newcomers are crypto prices. You can't imagine how many times I've heard friends new to crypto say "Bitcoin is expensive", I'm going to buy this altcoin - that's just a Dollar. Because it's cheaper and if it achieves the same price as Bitcoin, I'm going to be a millionaire." Well, here's the deal. The way to assess the relative value of a cryptocurrency, isn't its price. Instead you should be more concerned about its market cap. In short, this market cap number is just the number of coins circulating for that cryptocurrency multiplied by the price. It gives you a way better grasp of how cryptocurrencies are valued relative to each other. The two sites I recommend for checking out that are Coingecko.com and coinmarketcap.com. The point to take away here is that if a cryptocurrency is priced at just a few cents a coin, it doesn't mean it's cheap or you are necessarily bagging yourself a bargain, so be aware of that. Now that you know these cold hard crypto truths, do you still want to get involved in those crypto markets? If so, there are a few things you need to do to prepare. I should point out that nothing is stopping you from buying that crypto right now, but remember I talked about all those hackers and bandits out there trying to steal people's crypto? Well, we need to create our own version of Fort Knox before buying it. I mean if you bought a bar of gold and left it on the street, would you really expect it to be there in 30 minutes? Of course not. So I'm now going to share five steps that you need to take to help ensure that you can store your crypto safely. First, you should grab yourself a pen and paper. Put simply, if you write down all your crypto logins, passwords and seed phrases on a bit of paper, it cannot be hacked by some random computer wizard on the other side of the World. I don't mean to sound paranoid but it would be a good idea to make copies of this sensitive information and store it in different locations. For example, one copy can be hidden in your sock drawer and another copy stored in a safe deposit box across town. That way, if your house burns down you won't lose access to your crypto. A few other tips in terms of storing these critical details safely, is to put those important bits of paper in sealed ziploc bags. That way if you have a leak in your home, those crypto passwords should be safe. And finally, you might want to protect yourself against that house guest or cleaner randomly stumbling upon the keys to your crypto fortune. To do that, you might want to disguise those details by getting yourself a UV pen and black light. This way, that piece of paper looks like it doesn't have anything on it. So that means that almost anyone finding the keys to your crypto kingdom, is not going to know what it is they're looking at. Step two is to be aware that hackers are not like that kid at school who guess the password to your laptop. Manually guessing passwords is old hat. Instead they use what is termed a brute force attack, where they'll throw a database of passwords at your account in the hope that one works. So what is the defense against these brutes on the other side of the World trying to brute force your accounts? Well, having super long passwords with numbers, capital letters and special characters significantly increases the number of combinations that a bot needs to try to guess your password correctly. With the password cracking solutions widely available right now, that hacker might have to wait thousands of years before being able to guess that strong password. But how do you take your password security game to the next level? Well for every crypto account I would recommend that you use a different password. That means that if someone gets their hands on one, they can't access the others. Also some people like to take shortcuts by using password managers but these are also risky in the sense that if hackers can get access, they have the keys to your crypto kingdom. Back in 2017 there was even a situation where a crypto YouTuber had his Evernote hacked on live stream and watched his crypto flood out. Moving on, the next step is to make sure that your computer doesn't have any dodgy viruses or key loggers installed. Maybe you've clicked a link on a questionable website in the past and your computer is compromised with a key logger. If that happened, then a hacker can get all your passwords as you type them in on your keyboard. You can see if there's anything nasty lurking on your computer by using a free virus scanner like Malwarebytes. Install it and run a virus scan just to make sure all is good in the hood. The fourth step is to make sure your phone is secure. You will after all want to be securing all of your exchange accounts with two-factor authentication. A classic newbie mistake is to use SMS-based two-factor authentication. This is actually quite risky due to what is termed a sim-swap attack. This is basically when a thief calls your mobile operator and convinces them to port your number over to their phone. Once that's done they're able to receive your two-factor pin and reset your passwords. Users have literally had millions in crypto stolen from through these sorts of attacks. So what's the solution? Well, you'll want to install an authenticator app that generates one-time pins locally on the device. It basically binds itself to the exchange server and cannot be overtaken. There are a number of apps that do this including Google authenticator, Authy and Microsoft's authenticator. These basically generate a new six digit code every 30 seconds, which needs to be keyed into a computer to access your exchange account. My fifth step is to create a new email address that you'll only use for crypto stuff. After all, you've probably been using that same email address since you were 12 right? That means there are probably thousands of people out there that know it. My personal preference is Proton Mail. They're encrypted and hence much more secure than your standard email service providers, so head on over to protonmail.com and create a fresh email account just for crypto exchanges or wallets. The benefit of a new email address is that you make it harder for anyone to access your crypto accounts if they can somehow hack your personal email. You also have the added benefit of being able to segregate your personal emails from crypto related ones. Don't use your full name or surname in the Proton Mail account. It cuts out one additional breadcrumb that the hackers could use to identify you. Once you've got all that security set up and out of the way, you'll need a wallet to store that crypto safely. I know there are a lot of really safe exchanges out there and that you may be nervous about personally storing your cryptocurrency. But what you need to understand is that crypto kept on an exchange is nothing more than an IOU. You don't hold the keys and if the exchange was ever to get hacked, you could be left holding the bag. That's why if you're going to be storing a sizeable amount of crypto, I would recommend that you self-custody it and store it in an offline wallet. Better yet, you're going to want to get yourself a hardware wallet.

These hardware wallets cost anywhere between sixty Dollars and a hundred and eighty Dollars, however for the best crypto security money can buy, that seems like a more than reasonable price. When setting up your hardware wallet, you'll get 24 seed words presented to you. You'll certainly want to write these down on that important piece of paper I mentioned earlier. Basically, if you lose or damage your device you can use those seed words on a new hardware wallet to regain access to your crypto. Those seed words will work with any BIP 39 enabled crypto wallet so even if Tresor or Ledger goes out of business you can still access your funds. In short, if you're investing a few thousand Dollars into those crypto markets, then getting yourself a hardware wallet is probably the best decision you can make. That price is a small one to pay for peace of mind. Now if you've followed all those steps, you should have that piece of paper with all your important bits of crypto info on it. Got your crypto email set up, have your crypto wallet and secured your computer and phone. So you have all those security precautions set up and are now ready for the final step and that would be buying that crypto. The best way to buy crypto for you will depend on a variety of factors like which country you're based in, the specific cryptocurrencies you want to buy and the payment option you want to use. However, if you're based in Europe or countries like the UK, Canada, Singapore or Switzerland, the easiest way I found to buy crypto with a bank account is by using the Swissborg app. the bad news for anyone based in the US is that you cannot use Swissborg. On Swissborg you can buy popular cryptocurrencies like Bitcoin or Ethereum and a few more exotic cryptos like Engine coin too. So how do you buy that crypto? Well, click download app and you'll be taken to the app store. Install the app on your phone and open it up. On the home screen you'll see a big "get started" button. Click that, then you'll be asked to enter your mobile number. Next you'll be sent an SMS message with a six-digit code. Pop that in. Secure your Swissborg app with a four-digit pin and confirm it. Then you'll have to agree to Swissborg's terms of use and privacy policy. Click the slider to agree and bash the next button. Then you'll be asked to key in your name, date of birth and nationality. You'll then be asked to enter your email. Then you'll have to verify your email address. Click the mail icon to be taken to your inbox. Smash that verify email address button, you'll then see a green tick saying your email address has been verified and you'll need to click that open Swissborg app button to be taken back in. When back in the app you'll need to whack your postcode in there to find your address. Alternatively, you can enter your address manually. You'll then have to answer questions about your investment experience, employment status, occupation and your source of funds. Then it's time to verify your identity. Click the next button to get started with that. You'll then be told to find an ID document and get ready to take a selfie. Select the ID document you want to submit for verification. Next, you'll have to give Swissborg access to your camera. Hit that to enable camera button. Then just take a photo of that passport or other ID document and take that selfie. Once you have that, you're ready to deposit on Swissborg. To do that, click portfolio and hit that deposit button. The native currency of your country will be displayed here so click that currency. Finally, you'll see Swissborg's bank details. Log into your online banking and use those Swissborg details to make a payment. The really important thing to remember here is to use that random reference number in your transaction so your deposit can be matched to your Swissborg account. Once you've processed your payment from your bank account, sit back and relax and wait for that money to hit your Swissborg account. Then the deposit goes through, you're ready to buy your crypto. Click marketplace in the app and select the crypto you want to buy. You to select Bitcoin for example. Next you need to select what balance you want to buy that Bitcoin from. Because you have deposited fiat money, you'll want to click that. Then just key in the amount of Bitcoin you want to buy and click next. Finally, you'll be quoted a final price. Just confirm your purchase and congratulations, you've bought that crypto. It's also important to note that this process is basically the same to buy any cryptocurrency supported by

Swissborg.

Now that you've bought that crypto, you'll want to withdraw it to your hardware wallet to keep it safe. To do that, look at your portfolio and click on the crypto you want to withdraw. On the bottom right corner of the screen you'll see a send button. Click that and finally you'll see a field to enter your address that you've generated from your hardware wallet. Copy and paste it, double check it matches, and click next to send that crypto to your hardware wallet. Of course you can also send that Bitcoin or Ethereum to another exchange to trade them for more exotic altcoins and that's it. It's really that simple to buy crypto on Swissborg. But where is the best place to buy crypto if you're from the US? Well, the two most popular options are Binance US and Coinbase Pro. For both those options you're going to want to secure your account with 2FA so just as well you have that sorted already. Chances are you've heard of some hot new altcoin that you want to get your hands on. Let's say you want to buy injective protocol and are wondering which exchange you can buy it on. Well, you can find that out by hopping over to Coingecko or Coinmarketcap and searching for that hot altcoin. Once you've done that you'll be taken to the cryptocurrencies information page. Click the markets button and that will bring up all the different exchanges it's listed on. Then you can see there that you probably want to get a Binance account set up to buy INJ. You can use this method to work out which other exchanges you'll need to open an account in order to get that exotic crypto you have your eye on. If you want my personal opinion I find most of the coins that I'm looking for on Binance. It also supports regular fiat deposits but there are a few more steps required to get your fiat sent here when compared with Swissborg. You will need a Binance account either way if you want to buy those exotic altcoins. That's my ultimate beginner's guide to buying crypto. I know there was a lot to take in there and I might have scared you off from getting into crypto, however I think it's best to be brutally upfront about how things are. That way people can decide for themselves if all of this is for them. There are a lot of other great methods also to buy crypto but wanted to share with you the ones that are the fastest and easiest.

Chapter 3 - Kusama VS ThorChain

Take a minute to think about how you found out about that next best cryptocurrency. Chances are you either read about it in a crypto news article or noticed that it was one of the top performing cryptos in the past day or week on a site like Coingecko. The problem is that many promising cryptocurrencies fall through the cracks of these common methods of discovery. Kusama and ThorChain are prime examples of these. Both projects seem to have some serious utility, partnerships and community engagement, yet neither of the two has really made the crypto headlines. Even though KSM and Rune have both seen a 10x increase in price over the past six months, these gains seem to have been gradual enough to go unnoticed on daily and even weekly price leader boards. So in this chapter I'll be taking a close look at Kusama and ThorChain to see if there is more to these projects than meets the eye. Are KSM and Rune too crypto diamonds? Kusama was created by DR Gavin Wood who is also one of the co-founders of Ethereum. If the name sounds familiar that's because Gavin is also the founder of Polkadot. Kusama is referred to as a "canary network". This is a reference to the canary bird which was used by coal miners as an early warning signal for toxic gases in the air underground. To that, end Kusama exists as a means of testing the Polkadot network under real economic conditions and almost every feature that will ever be added to Polkadot, will first be tested on Kusama. That said, calling Kusama a Polkadot test net is not entirely accurate, because unlike regular test nets Kusama is intended to exist as its own network long after Polkadot is finished. Gavin expects both projects to evolve differently. Given that Kusama is focused around experimenting with economic incentives and pushing the network to the limit. While R&D stands for research and development on Polkadot on Kusama R&D stands for risk and danger. Kusama was soft launch in august 2019 and officially went live at the end of October that same year. this rollout served as a dry run for Polkadot's own main net launch which took place between May and August of 2020. When it comes to what's under the hood, Kusama is basically a carbon copy of Polkadot with a few key differences. For starters. Kusama's code has not been audited. Kusama's governance process is also four times faster than Polkadot's to allow for faster upgrades to the network. On Polkadot 1 percent of any unused treasury funds is burned whereas on Kusama, 0.2 percent of any unspent treasury funds go to the members of Kappa Sigma Mu. Kappa Sigma Mu is an "economic game to incentivize users to join a society that coordinates around whatever the rules are decided to be". The current rules dictate that to become a member of Kappa Sigma Mu, you must get a permanent tattoo of the Kusama bird. If you're wondering why anyone would be crazy enough to get a tattoo to join a crypto society, it's because that 0.2 percent of treasury rewards works out to around over 225,000 dollars per month. Since there are currently only 50 members of Kappa Sigma Mu, that means 4,500 Dollars per member per month. Not surprisingly, Kusama's crypto society made the news last year but it seems to have been the only time Kusama has been in the spotlight ever since the project launched in 2019. Unlike Polkadots Dot, Kusama's KSM never underwent a 100x redenomination. This means KSM's initial supply is still just 10 million. Around 9 million KSM is currently in circulation, however since 50% of KSM's supply is currently being staked, this works out to an actual circulating supply that is closer to 4.5 million. Speaking of staking, KSM has an inflation rate of about 7.5 percent per year which is not bad as far as inflationary cryptocurrencies go. It's also worth pointing out that any staked KSM has a seven day unlock period. This means, if and when KSM goes parabolic, the KSM that is being staked won't be making it to the exchanges right away, which could supercharge any positive price volatility. On the other hand, most of KSM supply seems to be held by just a dozen accounts; with the largest wallet holding nearly 800,000 KSM. Although that's only 8 percent of KSM's initial supply, it's nearly 20 percent of KSM circulating supply. Dumping even just half of the KSM in that wallet could seriously suppress a parabolic move. Still, KSM has one big advantage over many other altcoins from a technical analysis perspective, because this is KSM's first bull run, there are no previous price points to serve as resistance. Moreover, even though KSM currently has a price tag of over 110 Dollars, it still has a market cap of less than a billion Dollars, which means there is still a lot of room to grow. Besides KSM's tokenomics, there is another reason why I'm bullish on Kusama. Polkadot is supposed to begin rolling out its Parachain loan offerings sometime in 2021. This is Polkadot's way of figuring out which project is worthy of a Parachain slot on Polkadot's relay chain. As far as I can tell, the Polkadot team is planning to pilot these Parachain loan offerings on Kusama first. This means that some or possibly even all the projects that are currently competing to launch on Polkadot, will make their debut on Kusama. Although many of these projects will eventually transition to Polkadot, Kusama is where all their users will be until that day comes. In short, Kusama may soon host a substantial amount of the users, developers and projects in Polkadot's ecosystem. albeit for a limited time. Therefore I reckon that's going to have one hell of an effect on the price of KSM. But that's not all. Remember that Polkadot's relay chain has a limit of 100 Parachain slots. Every project is going to need its own Parachain. What will happen to the projects that didn't make the cut for Polkadot? Well, they'll go to Kusama. If that wasn't bullish enough, Gavin Wood has noted on many occasions that the team plans to bridge Kusama and Polkadot. Given that their networks are basically identical, this bridge sounds more like a merge. Does this mean that Kusama could grow to become just as big as Polkadot? From where I'm standing, it's a no-brainer.

Now let's see where ThorChain is headed. ThorChain was founded in the fall of 2018 by nobody. ThorChain has no founder, no CEO and apparently no concrete team either. Instead, the developers working on ThorChain are self-organized. This sketchy origin story and setup is part of why we haven't seen much about ThorChain in the news. On the bright side, ThorChain's code has been audited multiple times. ThorChain is a cross-chain liquidity protocol. This means that ThorChain makes it possible to trade different types of cryptocurrencies without the use of a centralized exchange. These swaps are lightning fast and cost next to nothing. That said, ThorChain is technically not a decentralized exchange. ThorChain is intended to be the backend protocol for decentralized exchanges like Uniswap. So, how does it work? Well, ThorChain uses a proof-of-stake blockchain that was built using the Cosmos SDK. You can think of ThorChain as being a middle layer that makes it possible to swap between cryptocurrencies on different blockchains like Bitcoin and Ethereum. How ThorChain works is pretty complicated. Decentralized exchanges rely on liquidity pools to execute trades. Each liquidity pool on DEX is like Uniswap consists of two assets like USDC and Eth. The price of each asset is determined by the ratio of the assets in the pool. For example, if there are 10 000 USDC and 10 Eth in a pool then each Eth is worth 1,000 Dollars. When someone buys one Eth for 1000 USDC, this increases the amount of USDC in that pool and reduces the amount of Eth which gives the remaining 9 Eth a higher price. ThorChain takes this idea to the next level by creating a series of liquidity pools, consisting of a cryptocurrency from any blockchain and the Rune token. As with regular DEX protocols, anyone can provide liquidity to these

ThorChain liquidity pools and earn interest on those funds and arbitrage traders can profit by taking advantage of any discrepancies in the market price of the assets in those liquidity pools. A network of anonymous nodes on the ThorChain blockchain hold the assets in these liquidity pools in various faults and watch for signals from the two blockchains involved to execute the desired transaction. For example, if I wanted to swap BTC to Eth using ThorChain, I would send my BTC to the appropriate vault, along with some Rune for fees. ThorChain nodes would see this transaction and send me Eth from the appropriate vault to my Ethereum address. Keep in mind, that this is what is going on behind the scenes. The front end DEX I would use to actually execute this transaction, would make this a seamless process. To ensure the ThorChain nodes don't steal from the vaults which hold the assets belonging to the liquidity pools, they have to stake at least 1 million Rune to run a node which is currently around 4 million Dollars. If ThorChain nodes attempt to steal from the vaults they have access to, they face extremely severe slashing penalties. To prevent any sort of large-scale coordinated attack on the network, Rune's tokenomics are designed such that the value of that rune being staked is always significantly greater than the total value on the ThorChain protocol. This is an extremely watered-down explanation of how ThorChain actually works. Interestingly enough, Rune is actually a BEP2 token on the Binance smart chain, which was also built using the Cosmos SDK. ThorChain held an initial decentralized exchange offering IDO of their Rune token on the Binance DEX, which took place a few months earlier in July 2019. Although 20 million Rune were allocated for this sale, only 7 million Rune was sold and the rest were burned. With a price tag of just over 3 cents, the Rune IDO raised just over 200,000 Dollars. Some months prior to the IDO, ThorChain had managed to raise just over 3 million Dollars between their seed sale and private sale by selling 100 million Rune. 60 million Rune tokens were allocated to community reserves, and 65 million rune tokens went to operational reserves. The team and advisors get dibs on 50 million Rune and over 220 million Rune have been set aside for liquidity providers and ThorChain nodes. All of these tokens have vesting schedules. When you add all these tokens together you get 500 million which is the maximum supply of Rune. While I'm generally not a fan of these sorts of token allocations, ThorChain has been remarkably transparent in pointing out which wallets are holding these rune tokens and even publishes monthly treasury reports on their medium, which detail how those tokens are being spent, if at all. You can actually use Coingecko to creep these Rune addresses yourself. This rally seems to have been started with the release of BEPSwap which is said to be the Uniswap of Binance chain, and is also apparently the first DeFi application to be built on the Binance chain. Given that BEPSwap has only processed around 8 million Dollars in daily trading volume, it doesn't seem that it will be competing with Uniswap anytime soon. But, what if I told you that it's not intended to. According to ThorChain's documentation, BEPSwap will eventually be replaced by the Asgardex which is described as a censorship resistant desktop client that will be the main portal into the system. That system isn't just going to be Binance chain either. The Devs at ThorChain are working on multiple chain integrations of their protocol with Bitcoin and Ethereum and they seem to be making some serious progress. What's more, is that ThorChain is also coming close to supporting privacy coins like Monero that are slowly being delisted from centralized cryptocurrency exchanges. Monero developers have been looking for ways to swap XMR with other cryptocurrencies without a centralized exchange for years. ThorChain's market cap is nearly a billion Dollars with Binance chain support alone. It might be impossible to estimate just how much value these integrations will add, once they go live. This all begs the question; who is behind this project? Well, this is going to be some speculation. The CEO of Binance explained that centralized exchanges are doomed to fail. Primarily because the intense competition between them means a race to the bottom in terms of exchange fees. Binance has evolved to become more of an ecosystem than a simple cryptocurrency exchange and the recent reveal of Binance pay is no exception. The total value locked in DeFi applications on the Binance chain has likewise been growing rapidly and it seems like Binance is shoving BNB on anyone's throat whenever they can. While it's quite obvious that Binance's relentless ecosystem expansion and BNB shilling is mainly because they have their hands in the honeypot. Is there another motive at play here? My evidence for this is a Forbes article from October 2020 that some of you may remember hearing about. The title says it all; "leaked Tai Chi document reveals Binance's elaborate scheme to evade Bitcoin regulators". If this Tai Chi document is to be believed this suggests that he is not a fan of regulations. That's not a far-fetched assumption to make, given that he works in cryptocurrency full-time. Imagine you run the largest cryptocurrency exchange in the World. You know centralized exchanges are doomed to fail and let's say you also want a way to get around regulations. What do you do? Well, you don't want to change your front end. That would scare away users. The ideal solution would be to swap out your back end with a DEX protocol. This protocol would need to be interoperable. It would need to be cheap, it would need to be fast and it would need to be capable of supporting every cryptocurrency in existence including privacy coins. Binance might be behind ThorChain. Just think about it; an anonymously founded project with almost no funding or community suddenly launches its token on the Binance chain. It manages to get many anonymous nodes from all around the World to participate on a network with insanely high barriers to entry to run a protocol that just so happens to be the perfect solution to the woes of the largest cryptocurrency exchange. Conspiracy theory or prophecy? We'll see.

Chapter 4 - Cardano VS Polkadot

2021 is going to be the year of smart contract blockchains. Not counting Tether half of the top 10 cryptocurrencies by market cap are smart contract compatible and these projects are all seeking the current leader; Ethereum. Of these large-capped smart contract cryptos, there are two which stand out as the most likely successors to the throne. I am of course speaking about Cardano and Polkadot. These two have seen an unprecedented amount of development and adoption over the past year, and they are consequently neck and neck in the rankings by market cap. Both Polkadot and Cardano are also on the verge of releasing major updates to their networks. This has many wondering which of the two projects will triumph as the true alternative to

Ethereum in 2021. So in this chapter I will be comparing Cardano and Polkadot and reveal which one has the best chance of becoming the next hotbed for smart contracts and decentralized cryptocurrency applications. When it comes to comparing cryptocurrency projects there are a lot of different metrics you can use. Given the size and complexity of both Cardano and Polkadot, I'm not going to get super technical. Instead, I'm going to stick to metrics that everyone can understand, starting with the least technical metric of all; comparing the founders of both projects. Dr Gavin Wood is the founder of Polkadot. He's a computer scientist and holds a PHD in human computer interfacing. Gavin is also the founder of the Web3 foundation, a Swiss non-profit which oversees the development of Polkadot and is the founder of Parity technologies which is a for-profit software development company based in the UK. It is commissioned by the Web3 foundation to develop and maintain Polkadot. Charles Hoskinson is the founder of Cardano. He is a mathematician but does not have a PHD. Charles is also the founder of Input Output Hong Kong or IOHK for short, which is a for-profit software development company based in Hong Kong. IOHK and a Japanese for-profit software development company called Emurgo are commissioned by the Cardano foundation also a Swiss non-profit to develop Cardano. Charles does not hold any official title at the Cardano foundation, which sports five council members. By contrast, the Web3 foundation has only three council members and one of them is Gavin. Charles and Gavin also co-founded Ethereum with Vitalik Buterin and five others in 2013. Charles left Ethereum in June of 2014, 13 months before the Ethereum main net went live. This was apparently due to a disagreement between him and Vitalik about accepting venture capital funding, which Charles supported and Vitalik opposed. Gavin left Ethereum in January 2016 to deliver on the promises Ethereum could not, referring to the rollout of Ethereum 2.0, which had originally been scheduled to happen shortly after the Ethereum main net went live in 2015. Until his departure, Gavin had served as Ethereum CTO where he authored the Ethereum yellow paper, invented the solidity coding language and even coded the first functional version of Ethereum. Though both Gavin and Charles are incredibly brilliant, Charles seems to spend a lot more time engaging with the Cardano community, than Gavin does with the Polkadot community. More importantly, Gavin and Charles have radically different approaches to building their respective projects and this is a reflection of their own individual personalities. Everything that ends up on Polkadot, first goes through Kusama an unaudited clone of Polkadot. By contrast, everything that ends up on Cardano is peer-reviewed by some of the smartest people in the World before being tested and implemented. As far as technology goes, Cardano and Polkadot are both proof-of-stake blockchains. That said, they have notably different architectures which again seems inspired by the personalities and experiences of their founders. Given that Polkadot was invented to deliver on the promises Ethereum could not, Polkadot is strangely similar to Ethereum 2.0. Polkadot uses an elaborate hybrid consensus mechanism called Grandpa / Babe, which allows the network to process around 1,000 transactions per second. Gavin has noted that Polkadot has a theoretical upper limit of 1 million transactions per second with power chains and multi-threading. Polkadot is essentially an ecosystem of blockchains called Parachains, that are connected to Polkadot's core blockchain called the Relay chain. These power chains will host all the smart contracts and DAPps in Polkadot's ecosystem, and there will be an initial limit of 100 Parachains. Unfortunately it's not yet clear whether these Parachains will be interoperable at the outset which is going to be a key factor in the adoption of Polkadot once these Parachains start to go live later this year. In contrast to Polkadot, Cardano has a more original design. The Cardano blockchain has two layers; the Cardano settlement layer which keeps track of token balances and transfers, and the Cardano computation layer which runs all the smart contracts. Cardano uses a consensus mechanism called Ouroboros proof of stake, which allows the network to process a few hundred transactions per second. However, once the hydra scaling solution is implemented, Cardano will be able to process 1 000 transactions per second for every validator that's connected to the network. This means that Cardano would need 1,000 validators to match the speed of Polkadot in its final form. On that note Cardano still has a way to go before you can call it a finished product. We are only at stage two of five in Cardano's development roadmap, with the remaining stages set to occur in the next year or two. The next stage is set to go live in March of this year and will enable smart contracts on Cardano. Staking on Cardano and Polkadot is where things really start to get interesting. Starting with Cardano, there are currently over 1500 validators that are collectively staking over 70 percent of all ADA in circulation. Delegation can be done directly from the URI and Daedalus wallets and offers a return of around 5% per year in ADA. Polkadot has around 300 validators that are collectively staking over 60% of all Dot in circulation. Nomination which is Polkadot's version of delegation can be done using the Polkadot JS browser extension and offers a return of around 14% per year in Dot. You might be thinking Polkadot is the clear winner here and you'd be right were it not for one small detail. When you stake on Polkadot, that Dot has a 28 day unlocking period if and when you decide to withdraw. On Cardano, you can withdraw your ADA at any time you like. The fine print on Cardano's taking is that the first time you stake you will not earn any rewards for the first 20 days and will only be able to claim rewards after 25 days. After that initial 25 day period, you can stake and unstake as you please with no penalties. That said, staking on Cardano seems to be a bit risky as Daedalus and URI are not the most stable wallets out there, and any big updates to Cardano, can lead to technical issues for delegators. Despite these issues, Cardano is technically five times more decentralized than Polkadot in terms of validators, and Cardano explicitly intends to become the most decentralized cryptocurrency blockchain in existence. By contrast, Polkadot has an upper limit of 1000 validators. The most obvious difference between Cardano and Polkadot in this regard is the difference in their token supply. ADA has a current supply of around 31.8 billion with a maximum supply of 45 billion. Dot has a current supply of 960 million and an initial supply of 1 billion. Logically, the larger the supply the lower the value of the coin which is why Dot is worth 16 and ADA is worth 35 cents, even though both have similar market caps. You'd be surprised how often this basic economic fact flies over the head of retail investors. Dot is inflationary to the tune of about eight percent per year and this inflation is used to reward validators and nominators. That said, one percent of any dot that was not spent from the Polkadot treasury is burned every month. Even though ADA is not inflationary around 13.9 billion ADA will gradually be minted over the next two decades to pay for staking rewards, which works out to a functional inflation rate of around seven percent per year. ADA's supply dynamics are a bit more complicated than this. One big difference between Dot and ADA is token allocation. Just over 80 percent of ADA's initial supply of 31 billion is in the hands of the community compared to fifty percent for Dot. This is reflected in the account balances of both cryptocurrencies which revealed that ADA's supply is more equitably distributed, compared to the supply of Dot which is heavily concentrated in the top 100 wallets. Speaking of wallets, there are nearly 300 000 Cardano wallets compared to just under 110 000 Polkadot wallets. This is actually pretty solid considering Polkadot has been live for less than a year, while Cardano has been around since September 2017. This also gives dot an edge from a technical analysis perspective, since it does not have a significant previous all-time high where it could see some serious resistance. By contrast, ADA may get rejected around its previous highs of around 1.2 Dollars when the next altcoin cycle starts, because I'm sure there are more than a few investors who bought the top that want to make back their losses. As far as adoption goes, Polkadot seems to be the current leader. There are over 350 projects building on Polkadot, 17 of which are DAP-s. As far as I can tell there is currently only one DAPp building on Cardano and that's Bondly Finance but before Dot holders laugh their way to the bank, consider this; while Polkadot still seems to be building its bridge to Ethereum, Cardano finished its ERC20 converter in the fall of 2020 and demoed it in their October update. To say that it looks impressive, is an understatement. During this demo, the IOHK team noted they are ready to help Ethereum projects clone or migrate their projects to Cardano. Many of these can easily be done, given that the ERC20 converter allows you to burn the tokens on Ethereum to mint an equivalent amount on Cardano. Smart contract functionality for Cardano is set to come as early as March of 2021 with the release of Gogen. This will give Cardano a huge head start over Polkadot, which may not see any DAPps launching on it until the end of the year. This weight could even stretch into 2022, if the Polkadot team decides to test their Parachain auctions on Kusama first, which seems to be the plan. Moreover, each DAPp on Polkadot will need its own Parachain and there are only 100 slots available. This technically means that Polkadot will be limited to 100 DAPps. No such limit exists for Cardano. Before ADA holders get too excited, consider this. Although the number of DAPps on Polkadot will be limited, the Parachain loan offering mechanism will ensure that every single one of those DAPps is a game changer. These Parachain loan offerings will also make it possible to do ICOs in a unique way that seems to sidestep any existing regulations. Either that, or it'll put Polkadot in the crosshairs of regulators. Given everything I covered in this chapter, it's easy to see how both Cardano and Polkadot rank among the top 10 cryptocurrencies by market cap. I only just scratched the surface of what these are up to, but we have enough information to make a verdict about which one will become the next Ethereum. Even though, neither Charles Hoskinson nor Gavin Wood have control over their respective projects, who they are and how they conduct themselves, certainly has an impact. Charles may not have the same credentials as Gavin does, but Charles is calm, calculated and incredibly involved with the development of Cardano. This is a big part of why Cardano has such a large and engaged community. Polkadot also has a large community but for a very different reason. As a pioneer of smart contract technologies, Gavin seems to attract the same sort of forward-thinking developers that are building DAPps that create communities. In my estimation, this is what has made Polkadot so successful, thus far. Despite their radically different approaches to development, Cardano and Polkadot seem to be evenly matched as far as specs go, and whether you prefer one over the other, ultimately depends on what you value more in a crypto project. If you value decentralization, then you probably prefer Cardano. If you value staking rewards, then you probably prefer Polkadot. If you value interoperability then Cardano seems to be the winner. But, if you're on the hunt for the next 100x altcoin, you'll probably find it in Polkadot's enormous ecosystem. Until Polkadot starts plugging in those power chains though, any issues with Ethereum will probably send developers running across Cardano's ERC20 bridge for refuge. In terms of raw price potential, you could argue you're better off with ADA because it has a smaller price tag which will attract investment from inexperienced retail investors. However, you could just as easily argue that Dot will perform better because of the 28 day unlock period for the hundreds of millions of Dot that are currently being staked, which restricts the market ready supply. Then again, you could counter that claim with the fact that most dot tokens are concentrated in only a few dozen wallets. Any one of those could suddenly dump their dot and crash the price. Overall, these projects are so evenly matched that you may as well flip a coin when deciding which will outperform the other.

Chapter 5 - What happens when all Bitcoin are mined

There is a reason why Bitcoin is often referred to as digital gold. This is because like gold, Bitcoin has a maximum supply, and while gold has utility in electronics and medicine, Bitcoin has utility as a network that allows you to safely transfer and store value without a middleman. This combination of scarcity and utility is what gives gold and Bitcoin their incredible value. But there's one big difference between gold and Bitcoin and this is that Bitcoin relies on the creation of new Bitcoin to reward miners to process transactions on the network. When all the gold gets mined, it will still be possible to exchange it but what happens when all the Bitcoin is mined? Will the Bitcoin network grind to a halt and bring the entire cryptocurrency space crashing down with it?

How long do we have before this happens? Is there a solution to this problem? Well don't fear because in this chapter I will answer all these questions and more. You perhaps are quite familiar with Bitcoin but I need to make sure we're all on the same page. As such I'm going to start with a quick refresher on some of the relevant points. The first Bitcoin block was mined on the 3rd of January 2009 presumably by Bitcoin's creator Satoshi Nakamoto. Bitcoin's genesis block contained a hidden message which read The Times 3rd of January 2009; "Chancellor on brink of second bailout for banks" which was the headline in the London Times newspaper on that day. In addition to this message, Bitcoin's first block contained the first ever cryptocurrency mining reward of 50 BTC. The rationale behind having BTC coins at all, is that they serve as an economic incentive for miners to maintain the network. BTC is given as a reward for processing transactions, which are written to blocks on the Bitcoin blockchain. New BTC are issued every time a new Bitcoin block is mined. The Bitcoin code ensures that this happens roughly every 10 minutes by adjusting the mining difficulty, depending on how many miners there are. The Bitcoin block reward was 50 BTC until November 28 2012 when Bitcoin underwent its first halving, reducing the block reward from 50 BTC to 25 BTC. A Bitcoin halving happens every 210,000 blocks. Although this technically works out to four years, the actual figure is a bit different. The Bitcoin halvings are significant because the sudden reduction in new BTC supply they cause, is thought to eventually cause a spike in the price of BTC, assuming demand for BTC stays the same or increases after the halving. Case in point, the most recent Bitcoin halving happened in May of 2020 and it's quite clear that we're now in a bull market. These Bitcoin halvings aren't going to keep happening forever. That's because the maximum amount of BTC that can ever be mined is 21 million, and this limit is built into Bitcoin's code. It is likely that Satoshi Nakamoto chose this limit for mathematical reasons. It is also possible that he chose this limit based on the World's M1 money supply, which was around 21 trillion Dollars in 2009. If this is the case then it means Satoshi intended each BTC to eventually be worth one million Dollars. When will the last BTC be mined? Well if you've Googled this question before you probably got the same answer everyone else did which was the year 2140. If you think that seems a long time given the current circulating supply of BTC is around 18.6 million, you would be correct. When you dig deeper into the calculation used by most articles to come to this figure, you'll notice it assumes that Bitcoin undergoes a halving every four years, which is not entirely correct. They're not exactly four years apart. In fact, they're only about three years and nine months apart. Thankfully someone else did the maths on this and they found out that if you assume this three year and nine month gap continues, the last BTC will probably be mined at the end of 2078. When there's no more BTC to mine, there will be no more economic incentives for miners and the Bitcoin network will die, and since the entire cryptocurrency market is dependent on Bitcoin, every cryptocurrency will go to zero, said nobody ever. First off, Bitcoin dominance has been dropping like a rock since 2017, which suggests that BTC will not be the largest cryptocurrency by market cap in 2078. Meaning, the rest of the crypto market will not be as dependent on it anymore. Also, besides what the BTC miners get from each new Bitcoin block, they also earn fees as compensation for processing transactions. If you pop open a Bitcoin block explorer, you can actually see the amount of fees in BTC a miner earned from the block that they mined by subtracting the current BTC rewards from the total block reward. In this case, we can see that miners are earning anywhere between 0.5 to 1 BTC per block in transaction fees alone. Many people believe that by the time the BTC mining rewards run out, these transaction fees will be enough to sustain the Bitcoin network. There's just one problem with this hypothesis. Given that Bitcoin can only process around seven transactions per second, it's very unlikely that it's going to become the payment network that is used for micro transactions like buying a pack of gum at a grocery store. The transaction fees alone would be multiples of what you were spending. Bitcoin developers are very much aware of the growing cost of transaction fees and how they disrupt micro payments. It's why they've been developing layer 2 scaling solutions like the lightning network for years. The problem with layer 2 solutions like the lightning network is that they reduce the number of transactions that actually occur on the Bitcoin blockchain. Instead, they only submit transactions to the Bitcoin blockchain when a payment channel is opened and when it is closed. Fewer transactions mean that the fees for opening and closing these payment channels would have to be incredibly high for Bitcoin miners to remain profitable and operational. After all, they have to cover the cost of the hardware and electricity required to maintain the Bitcoin network. These high fees would then put pressure on layer twos like the lightning network to minimize the opening and closing of their payment channels, resulting in a vicious cycle that would either bankrupt Bitcoin miners or corrupt the Bitcoin network due to excessive reliance on less secure layer 2 solutions. Bitcoin maximalists will disagree, but it seems quite clear that Bitcoin's main stick is as a store of value, not as a currency network that's used for day-to-day transactions. As such, it is much more likely that BTC will seldom be moved around in the future, contrary to what Satoshi Nakamoto envisioned. This means that if Bitcoin is going to survive beyond the data that stops rewarding miners with BTC, it will need to be able to do so without relying on transaction fees. Here are a few solutions on the horizon. Sustaining a proof-of-work cryptocurrency network like Bitcoin requires a lot of computing power and a lot of electricity. These make up the bulk of the operating expenses of cryptocurrency miners around the World, and it's why a lot of mining farms flock to countries and regions with cheap energy, namely China and parts of north America. Even though the Bitcoin network is unlikely to survive on transaction fees alone, this is based on the assumption that the cost of cryptocurrency mining will be the same when we run out of BTC. But it is very likely that energy will become cheaper and technology will become more efficient in the coming decades. Although, green energy solutions are still very much in their infancy, green energy providers in the UK are actually using their excess power to mine cryptocurrencies. This makes their services even more profitable and allows them to expand their green energy operations. Much the humiliation of the fudsters' who claim that cryptocurrency mining is killing the planet. Furthermore, Bitcoin mining rigs are becoming more affordable and more efficient by the year. Cheap energy and efficient hardware would make it easy for Bitcoin miners to stay profitable, using transaction fees alone and it would even further decentralize Bitcoin as new miners join the network to get a share of those fees. Economic incentives aren't the only thing that could keep the Bitcoin network afloat either. Ever since companies like Microstrategy began accumulating Bitcoin as part of their treasury reserves, many have been speculating when the public sector will follow suit. It seems that it's only a matter of time given that the mayor of Miami recently considered investing 1 percent of the city's treasury reserves into BTC. If and when cities states and even governments begin holding BTC as part of their reserves, they will have all the incentive in the World to make sure the Bitcoin network remains secure and operational. If public institutions are holding BTC after the last one is mined, and they find out that Bitcoin miners are starting to shut off their mining rigs because they're not making profits, they would not hesitate to subsidize those miners or even start their own mining operations to sustain the Bitcoin network. Similarly, if enough people in a given country hold BTC and the Bitcoin network is at risk, they could pressurize their government to implement subsidies for Bitcoin mining farms to protect their wealth. These protectionist measures may not come from just the public sector either. If enough private companies start to hold large amounts of BTC, they too would have reason to rush in and make sure the Bitcoin network remains operational. This skin in the game principle is what motivates people to run Bitcoin nodes, which store copies of transaction histories on the Bitcoin blockchain to support the network's decentralization. There are over 6,400 Bitcoin nodes even though they do not earn any transaction fees or mining rewards for the valuable service they provide. Another possibility is that we could simply see the entire Bitcoin network migrate to a smart contract blockchain like Ethereum. Almost seven percent of Bitcoin circulating supply is currently on Ethereum as an ERC20 token as WBTC and RenBTC. This is thanks to something called "wrapping", which locks a cryptocurrency on its native blockchain to mint an equivalent amount of ERC20 tokens on Ethereum. The amount of wrapped BTC has increased substantially over the past year and this is for two reasons; first you can use wrapped BTC in various DeFi protocols to earn interest on your BTC. Second it's usually faster and cheaper to move WBTC around than actual BTC. It's not just Ethereum either. Cardano and Polkadot are expected to roll out their smart contract functionalities this year and Polkadot announced in October 2020 that they will be supporting wrapped BTC on their network in Q1 of this year as Polka BTC. By the time the BTC rewards run out, Ethereum, Polkadot and Cardano would be insanely decentralized. Meaning, there would be little to no issues as far as network security goes. The only challenge would be migrating all the BTC on the Bitcoin blockchain to Ethereum which is likely something that not every BTC holder would be willing to do. That said, it is very doable since BTC can be burned on the Bitcoin blockchain by sending it to a dummy address. These dummy addresses are the sorts of addresses that you've accidentally transferred funds to when you are still a crypto noob. An Ethereum smart contract could watch the transactions being sent to these dummy Bitcoin addresses and mint an equivalent amount of BTC as ERC20 tokens. There is of course one last solution on the table and that's to increase the supply of BTC. I know what you're thinking; I thought 21 million was a protocol defined limit and yes, you are right. However, it is technically possible to increase this limit. So long as there is consensus from the quote economic majority and that's not just 51% of miners. That includes all economic participants; miners, developers, users, merchants, the whole shebang. The overwhelming majority of these groups have to be in agreement about any significant change to the Bitcoin network for it to pass, even though it's ultimately the developers at companies like Blockstream that implement the changes to Bitcoin's code. If you're wondering why, consider the following. When part of the Bitcoin community wanted to increase Bitcoin's block size to accommodate more transactions, not everyone was on board with the idea. This resulted in a fork of the Bitcoin network in the summer of 2017. The new

Bitcoin blockchain with the larger block size became known as Bitcoin cash. Bitcoin cash actually forked again in November 2018 to spawn Bitcoin Satoshi Vision aka Bitcoin SV. Even though the economic stakeholders in Bitcoin's ecosystem that we see today would never designate a Bitcoin blockchain with a higher BTC supply as the real Bitcoin, this could potentially change in the coming years and decades. It is entirely possible that the maximum supply of BTC could someday be increased. As it turns out, Bitcoin has more than one way of surviving well past the day those BTC mining rewards run out. I find it crazy that this will probably happen in my lifetime, but the advancements we're going to see in the cryptocurrency space between now and then are going to be even crazier. After all, the crypto space isn't the only place where innovation is happening. Many of these new inventions are going to be relevant to the Bitcoin network and could potentially make it possible to create an entirely new economic model for cryptocurrency mining. This is going to be necessary because, I really don't see how the Bitcoin network could sustain itself on transaction fees alone and layer 2 solutions will not help at all with that issue. When it comes to payments, there is no shortage of competition in the cryptocurrency space and many of these competing projects do a much better job than Bitcoin. Bitcoin is a store of value and the public and private institutions are starting to see the light too. It would not surprise me in the slightest if we see a major city state or government list BTC among its reserve assets by the end of this year. Even when that news comes out it will be the final confirmation that the Bitcoin network is here to stay. Oddly enough, it seems that BTC coins are slowly but surely migrating to greener pastures. It is very likely that the majority of all existing BTC will be locked on smart contract blockchains like Ethereum, Polkadot and Cardano by the end of the decade. At the end of the day everything revolves around economic incentives and it is logical that people want to move their store of value assets to platforms where they can earn interest. As for increasing the maximum supply of BTC, that is just completely out of the question for the time being. Bitcoin is the most secure network in the World. It has millions of users, millions of miners and tens of thousands of the World's brightest minds working on it day and night. No amount of fun can change this fact.

Chapter 6 - Best and Must have Hardware Wallets

Are you a future crypto millionaire who's found that hot cryptocurrency which is going to take you to the moon? Well top marks on being a first-class crypto scientist, however here's the problem; realistically those legendary 100x games aren't likely to happen overnight. That means if you've picked that winner, you're probably going to have to wait a bit for those sorts of insane games to happen. But here's the question; are know-how crypto hodlers' just sitting around with that crypto waiting to be hacked? Of course not. So in this chapter I'm going to go over the safest crypto wallets that money can buy. I'm also going to share a few essential crypto tips when it comes to using these devices. To get started I should probably explain the different ways that you can store crypto and why I think that hardware wallets are your best bet. The truth is that most crypto newbies rock onto a crypto exchange buy that crypto and just leave it there. That is really convenient and is minimal hassle. But what's the problem with that approach? Well, if you do that, you won't actually hold your private keys. Instead, you're essentially the owner of an IOU issued by a company you first heard about 10 minutes ago. I must stress that crypto is still like the wild west with hundreds of new exchanges springing up every year. Let's just say that some of those have very questionable business practices or the exchange might simply be a front to collect your money before the crooks vanish into the Ether. Don't believe me? Well, that's allegedly what happened at Quadriga CX, the coin base of Canada. Even if you're fortunate enough to be keeping your coins on an honest exchange, there is one major threat, and that would be that exchange hacks are not exactly uncommon. After all, when there are literally hundreds of millions of Dollars lying around on exchanges, it's not surprising that they make a tempting target for hackers. Here are some examples. In 2020, Kucoin got hacked for a whopping 281 million Dollars. Just a few months later, EXMO lost six percent of all user funds on the exchange to a hack. Other shady exchanges might make it nearly impossible to get your coins off their exchange too. However, there are many legit exchanges out there. Here's the deal; even if you opt to use one of those top exchanges have you got full 100% certainty that they'll keep your crypto safe, sadly no one can. Sure, I'm comfortable keeping small amounts on the exchange but anything larger leaves me a tad worried. That's why so many crypto hodlers' in the space recommend that you store your coins in a wallet you control - self-custody. That way you control those private keys and are not reliant on that exchange middleman protecting your funds for you. The easiest way of doing that is by downloading a free wallet app on your phone or computer. These apps are super convenient and you do control those all-important private keys but here's the problem with those types of wallet. Those private keys are exposed every time you connect the internet which I imagine is pretty much all the time for those smartphone and computer users out there. Click on the wrong link, download a dodgy app by accident or get that other type of virus and that hacker could empty those crypto coffers in a flash. You could go low-tech and protect yourself against hackers by going for paper wallet route. Yet there are good reasons why this isn't exactly a popular option anymore. They're pretty inconvenient. Most people don't want to be printing out a new paper wallet for every transaction they receive, which means that many paper wallet users reuse the same address. Finally, if you're a butterfingers, then you could lose access to that crypto by simply spilling a cup of coffee over that precious piece of paper. Finally, you have hardware wallets. But what are they? Well, these wallets are physical devices that come in all manner of shapes and sizes. In short, they store your private keys in a way that the private key never leaves the device. Also each transaction needs to be validated on the device itself. All that matters as it means that your private keys are never exposed to your computer and by extension that scary outside World of would-be crypto thieves. It also means that if your computer has a virus or malware, you can still use these devices safely on that computer. So if you're wanting the best crypto security to guard that future fortune against remote attacks, then you are going to want to get a hardware wallet. With all that being said, hardware wallets do have two key vulnerabilities. The first is what crypto security experts named the deadly five Dollar wrench attack. It's actually a highly technical exploit that involves the use of really advanced piece of equipment. As an attacker all I need to do in order to get your crypto is to clobber you over the head until you give me your password. A low tech but pretty effective hack. What can you do to help protect yourself against that five Dollar wrench attack? Well, you don't want to be bragging to that girl you met a few minutes ago about all the crypto you have. Chances are they wouldn't be very impressed, anyhow and you also don't know who is listening in on that mad cryptoflex. Point is, that if no one knows that you own crypto then you can probably sleep well with that hardware wallet tucked under your pillow. The second potential vulnerability with hardware wallets is buying them from an unofficial supplier. This basically involves scammers on the likes of eBay or Amazon, sending you pre-programmed seed words on a poisoned device. The easy way to protect yourself from that nightmare is to buy directly from the hardware wallet company themselves. Now that you know all the ins and outs of crypto wallets it's time for the main event. Which is the best hardware wallet? Let's move on to my top five picks starting at the bottom. I will start with Ledger Nano devices as I am happily using them for years now. Firstly, I need to be straight up and say that to my knowledge there is nothing wrong with the security of Ledger devices themselves. But what you need to know is that Ledger suffered a data breach in mid-2020. It turns out that 270,000 customer home addresses, telephone numbers and names were released into the wild at the end of last year. That data dump also included around 1 million email addresses too. That all kick-started a slew of scam emails to Ledger customers trying to extort them for money. What's even scarier, is the thought of criminals using that list to five Dollar wrench attack anyone in their local area. The hardware wallets themselves are top notch, but this whole debacle has shaken my faith in Ledger keeping that all important private data secure. If you're willing to overlook that in discretion by Ledger, what hardware wallets have they got on the shelves over there? Well, the Ledger Nano S will set you back around 55 Pounds that's around 75 USD or 62 Euros. For that modest price point you'll have the ability to store 27 coins and more than 1500 tokens. All that is possible by using the Ledger live desktop app to manage those cryptocurrency accounts. That makes it simple to store, send and receive crypto. Still it is important for any would-be Ledger Nano S owner to know that only three to six applications can be stored on your device at once. What that means is that those with large portfolios stuff full of exotic altcoins, might get frustrated by having to constantly uninstall and reinstall apps to manage all those cryptos. So just be aware of that. You might be thinking that a capacity of just three or six apps is nowhere near enough. Well, it might not be as big an issue as you think. The reason why is that each separate blockchain has its own app. That means you can store any ERC20 token by just installing the Ethereum app. Also, staking for a bunch of coins is also supported. Moving on to security, there are no known hacks when it comes to the devices themselves so there is a solid record in that department. Another cool thing about Ledger is that it integrates with a host of Web3 wallets like

Metamask which are almost mandatory when it comes to dabbling in DeFi. If that's something you want to do then you might want to consider getting a Ledger. Who is the Ledger Nano S for? Well, it's for anyone that can see past the Ledger data breach and is only likely to use a handful of apps. The 55 pound price point will also appeal to the value hunters out there who want to store a vast array of coins. The Ledger Nano S was the original hardware wallet, but those interested in Ledger also have a newer shinier option to consider. That would be the Ledger Nano X. Some say the Ledger Nano X shows up the S when it comes to looks. I must say the bigger screen is pretty useful but how much does it cost? Well, a pretty eye watering 109 Pounds, 148 Dollars or 124 Euros. For that extra money, you get a bigger screen, better build quality and Bluetooth connectivity which allows you to use the device with the Ledger live app on your mobile. Finally those altcoin dabblers who have pushed crypto diversification to the limits, will be pleased to know that the Ledger Nano X can install up to 100 apps. Even the most hardcore altcoiner is unlikely to have to mess around with uninstalling and reinstalling apps. If you're considering a Ledger hardware wallet, then the question you should be asking is if all those additional features are worth paying double the price. Honestly, if I was forced to pick between the two types of Ledgers I'd probably go for the more economical Ledger Nano S and save that extra money. That being said, I do understand how the x could appeal to those that hold crypto portfolios with a overabundance of different coins. If you are going to be buying either Ledger device I would refrain from handing over any phone numbers. You should also use a separate email address from your main one. It's just an added precaution.

In the fourth spot I have Coldcard. This mid-tier option comes in at 120 dollars, 88 Pounds or 100 Euros. Why would you consider getting one? Well, it's safe to say that Coldcard is probably the most secure hardware wallet out there. That's due to a host of security features and these include some of the following; a duress pin which you can punch in if you're under attack from a five Dollar wrench wielding baddie. If you use that pin, then everything seems normal to the attacker, however what's really happened is that the Bitcoin key generated isn't your regular one with all your Bitcoin. Instead, a completely separate wallet is opens up. You can use that a bit like you would use a fake wallet to mislead muggers in the real World. If you're the kind of person who's not happy with misdirection and giving up a single Satoshi then you have another option. Coldcard also lets you set up a brick me pin, which fries the secure element on the device and renders it inoperable. A bit like a self-destruct button. Of course you will need your seed words to recover them but the hope is that the attacker doesn't have them. If the attacker tries to brute force your pin then Coldcard has an option for that as well. You get 13 attempts or the device gets fried. Another cool security feature is that you can operate this wallet completely air-gapped, basically completely unconnected to your PC. You can manage that Bitcoin and use the device by just plugging it into a power bank or power adapter. Finally, some people don't trust the randomness of seed word generators. With Coldcard, you can generate that seed phrase by using random dice rolls. I've not seen most of these kinds of security features implemented on any other hardware wallet. Also, what's awesome is that all code for Coldcard is open sourced so anyone can take a look and see if that code is legit. Essentially Coldcard is a bit like an upgraded Fort Knox for the 21st century. It sounds like a no-brainer but there are some drawbacks. The first is that this wallet only supports Bitcoin. Another drawback is that Coldcard security does come at the expense of ease of use. If you want to sign a BTC transaction, you'll need to create a partially signed Bitcoin transaction on your device before you can finally sign that transaction. That's pretty time consuming and irritating if you send a ton of BTC transactions. But who is Coldcard for? Well I'm going to say that this wallet is the most secure option I've seen. It's simply got a host of security features that I've yet to see elsewhere. Still, all that counts for nothing if you intend to store altcoins. Also, it's not the most straightforward wallet to use either. All that being said, if you have a massive stack of Bitcoin then you'll definitely want to consider this option.

At number three, I have Ellipal Tital. This is yet another air-gapped cold wallet and you can get your hands on one for 139 Dollars, 102 Pounds or 115 Euros. That might be the most expensive wallet I've brought up so far but it could well be worth that price. To start, the wallet is sealed to be dust and water jet proof. Also if anyone tries to force the wallet open to tinker with it, your keys will be deleted once a breach is detected, thus protecting your wallet against physical attacks. As the Ellipal Tital relies on the sole use of QR codes for data transfer, it is never connected to things like USBs, WiFi or Bluetooth. You want this to fully secure yourself against remote attacks. Unlike Coldcard, this wallet is also pretty easy to set up and use. It also supports over 7000 crypto assets too so the chances are that the coin you want to store is supported here. Ellipal Tital also allows you to stake your coins, earn interest, exchange or buy crypto through its apps too. There's a whole lot to like about this Ellipal Tital wallet. The one thing I would say is that it's relatively new and doesn't have the proven track record of market leaders like Ledger or Trezer. So, who is this wallet for? Well, anyone that wants an air-gapped wallet with multi-crypto support at a reasonable price.

Now it's time for my second pick and that has to be KeepKey. KeepKey was founded all the way back in 2015 and was acquired by Shapeshift in 2017. One of the main attractions of KeepKey is its insanely reasonable price point of 49 Pounds, 36 Pounds or 40 Euros. It's also got a significantly bigger screen than even that Ledger Nano X. Needless to say, it's also got full integration with Shapeshift. That means that this wallet essentially has a full crypto exchange contained inside. Pretty convenient if you want to trade crypto securely. The device itself is secured by a pin code and backed up with seed words. For a while, KeepKey did have a pin vulnerability. Basically, Ledger found a way to extract those pin codes from KeepKey wallets. This KeepKey vulnerability did require physical access to the device. It was also fixed pretty quickly by the KeepKey team with a firmware update. But, what about that all-important crypto support? Well, KeepKey allows you to store over 40 cryptocurrencies. That's not the widest selection however you can combine KeepKey with MyEtherWallet and store any ERC20 token so that's around another 1,000 cryptos right there. My main complaint with this hardware wallet is that some of those hot alt coins I hold are not supported which is a bit of a let-down. With all that being said how can you object with KeepKey at 49 Dollars. Basically, if you're looking to get your hands on a hardware wallet with a ton of features and at a modest price, then KeepKey certainly needs to be considered.

My final pick is Trezor. After the Ledger data breach, Trezor became my go-to hardware wallet of choice and is what I use to store my crypto now. But there are two types of Trezors. Well I'm going to look first at the latest Trezor model T first. This will set you back a staggering 159 Euros 190 Dollars or 140 Pounds. Like both Trezor models, the Model T is air gapped for 99% of the time. But if you want to use it, you'll have to plug it into your computer or phone with a USBC connector. An important thing to note is that Trezor mobile support doesn't extend to the cool kids with iPhones. I can safely say that I find these devices are the easiest ones to set up and use. That's a massive plus for anyone new to crypto. In other good news, the Trezor Model T boasts support for the most cryptos. How many exactly? Well, 1,615 to be precise. So if you've found that hidden 1000x gem, then Trezor is your best shot at storing it. The Model T also comes with a bigger screen than the other type of Trezor. Its color has touch screen functionality and the device also supports micro SD cards. If those sorts of features have value to you, then that's certainly something to consider. Another cool thing with both types of Trezor is that they integrate with a free wallet called Exodus. The reason why I think that's a big deal is that Exodus not only looks stunning, but it is the go-to option that I point my friends towards when they're sitting on the fence when it comes to getting a mobile wallet. That integration gives Exodus wallet users that option to upgrade their security with Trezor. Essentially the Trezor Model T is the ideal hardware wallet for anyone who values ease of use and support for the widest possible range of coins. With all that being said, I think the Trezor 1 is the best choice out there for most people. It doesn't have that flashy color touchscreen or micro SD card support, but the Trezor 1 only sets you back 49 Euros, 59 Dollars or 43 Pounds. You could literally buy three Trezor 1-s for the same price of a Model T. Pretty much everything else that I've said about the Trezor Model T applies to the Trezor 1, however there is one major difference when it comes to supported coins. The Trezor Model T supports cryptos like XRP, Cardano, EOS, and Monero while the Trezor 1 doesn't so if you're hodling' any of those to the moon, then you might want to opt for a Model T instead. If you really want to spend that extra 100 Euros on the flashier Trezor Model instead, that's fine but I imagine most people out there would be better off saving that extra 100 Euros or so and opting for the cheaper model instead. So who is the Trezor for? Well, anyone who wants an easy way to protect their crypto against remote attacks at a keen price point and wants the option to store around 1600 different cryptocurrencies.

Chapter 7 - How to Reduce ETH Gas Fees

You've perhaps aware that the Ethereum high gas fees have made the network almost unusable. Once upon a time the side effects of high gas fees were only felt by those using DeFi protocols and decentralized exchanges like Uniswap, where a simple swap could cost you over 100 Dollars in gas. Even centralized exchanges are charging upwards of 40 Dollars in fees to withdraw ERC20 stable coins like USDT and USDC. I also heard recently that someone paid over 120 Dollars in gas just to send their Aave tokens to another Ethereum wallet address. So in this chapter I'm going to explain how Ethereum gas works, how you can reduce gas fees and how you can even profit from these rising gas costs. Like every other cryptocurrency, the Ethereum network has transaction fees known as gas. Ethereum gas fees are measured in a unit called a gigawei or Wei for short. Wei is the smallest denomination of the Eth cryptocurrency. One Wei represents one quintillionth of an Eth and one Wei is one billionth of an Eth. These gas fees are paid to Ethereum miners to ensure that your transaction gets processed. In other words, to ensure that transaction is included in the next Ethereum block. It's often said that Ethereum miners set the gas fees but this isn't entirely correct. Ethereum miners vote to set something called the gas limit, which is how much gas can be included in each Ethereum block. Back in the day, this gas limit was around three million Wei per Ethereum block. Today the gas limit is over 12 million Wei. If you're wondering why miners would increase the gas limit, it's because it allows the Ethereum network to squeeze in more transactions per block. This theoretically makes the Ethereum network slightly cheaper and faster for users without sacrificing transaction fee profits for Ethereum miners. The problem is that increasing the gas limit also raises the barrier to entry for new Ethereum miners and Ethereum nodes, which threatens the decentralization of the Ethereum network. Increasing the gas limit also doesn't change the fact that there is limited transaction space in each Ethereum block. Even with a higher gas limit, if the Ethereum network is busy enough, it means you're going to be paying a premium to get the Ethereum miners to include your transaction in the next Ethereum block. A few hundred Wei in gas fees isn't much when the price of Eth is low but when Eth is pushing past new all-time highs like it is now, it can cost a few Dollars. Naturally, the more complex the transaction, the more Ethereum gas you're going to need to pay to get that transaction included in the next block. It currently costs hundreds of Dollars in Eth to interact with most DeFi protocols. This is essentially limited Ethereum DeFi to people with very deep pockets. That said, there are many ways you can reduce these insane Ethereum gas fees. Almost every single Ethereum wallet in existence lets you set your own personal gas limit before sending a transaction. The gas limit you see in wallets like MyEtherwallet and Metamask is different than the gas limit set by miners in each Ethereum block I mentioned. Your personal gas limit is essentially the maximum amount of Wei that you're willing to pay for that transaction to go through. A lot of Ethereum wallets will give you the option to send your transaction at a slow speed, regular speed or fast speed. Most of the time, the gas fees they give you for each of these transaction speeds are not always up to date. That's no fault of their own. The amount of gas you need to get a transaction through actually fluctuates from block to block. That's why the first thing you should do before sending an Ethereum transaction from a wallet is to check a website like Eth gas station to see the most up-to-date gas fees. You can download their browser extension plugin so you always have those gas fees handy. Once you know what the actual fee is for the transaction you want to send, you can manually enter the amount of Wei you're willing to pay for that transaction in the Ethereum wallet you're using. If you want to go one step further, you can check out a cool website called https://txstreet.com/ which actually shows you how those gas fees are changing from block to block in real time. Setting your own custom gas limits using these tools can reduce your Ethereum gas costs by up to 30 percent. Another similar way to reduce gas fees is to transact during

Ethereum's quiet hours. These are between 8 and 11 PM UTC. Ethereum gas costs can be up to 50 percent cheaper during that time frame. Before you even make an Ethereum transaction, you should be asking yourself if it really needs to be done right this minute. Unless you're executing a mind-melting arbitrage trade using a flash loan, sticking to the bare minimum gas limit you see on each gas station during Ethereum's quiet hours is probably the way to go. Just be careful not to put too little gas or else your transaction could get stuck. This is actually a lot worse than it sounds because you'll not be able to send any other transaction from that wallet until that stuck transaction has been pushed through with additional gas or reversed. If you decide to brute force the transaction with additional gas, you have to make sure you're using at least 10 percent more than the previous fee, regardless of the current gas costs.

If for some reason you've changed your mind and want to reverse that transaction, you have to find the failed transaction on Ether scan, navigate to the additional details and find the nonce number for that transaction. Then you simply send zero Ethereum to your own Ethereum address using the current gas price with the nonce number as reference. This will replace the stuck transaction effectively cancelling it and making it possible to send new transactions again. Speeding up or cancelling stuck transactions can all be easily done through Metamask. If you want to save gas while simultaneously profiting from high gas fees on Ethereum, then gas tokens are the way to go. The first gas token was invented in late 2017 by a group of blockchain researchers from various top-tier universities around the World. Gas tokens take advantage of a function on Ethereum called the "storage refund". This is basically where the

Ethereum network refunds a portion of the Eth used for gas in a smart contract when some of the data inside of it are deleted. The storage refund function exists to motivate developers to free up space on the Ethereum blockchain, which stores all the data generated by smart contracts. Gas tokens are essentially junk data inside a dummy smart contract that can be destroyed in exchange for Ethereum gas. The basic idea behind gas tokens is that you mint them when the cost of gas is low and then burn them to reduce gas costs by 50 percent, when the cost of gas is high. Gas tokens can also be sold for a profit instead on decentralized exchanges such as Uniswap and gas tokens are a big part of why many cryptocurrency wallets that used to offer Ethereum gas or gas subsidies stopped doing so in the fall of 2020. Clever users realized that they could use the free Ethereum gas being provided by these wallets to mint gas tokens that could be sold for a handsome profit further down the road. Although the original gas token is unaudited and seems to have some sketchy tokenomics, an improved version of the original gas token called the "Chi gas token" was created by DEX aggregator in June of 2020. The Chi gas token has pulled an impressive 20x since the fall and continues to rise in accordance with Ethereum's gas fees. The Chi gas token can be minted using Eth on the 1-inch exchange and you can mint up to 140 Chi at a time. Before you run off and fill up your bags, be aware that minting these gas tokens ironically requires a lot of gas. To just break even on the minting the Dollar value of Chi would theoretically have to grow by more than 50 percent. Luckily, you can set limit orders on 1 inch exchange to automatically sell that Chi when it's the higher price you're shooting for if you're buying Chi to save on gas cost you can use it on the one inch exchange or curve finance to save up to 40 on gas. If you need to use gas tokens in other DeFi protocols then you'll have to use the original gas token. The last thing you can do to save on Ethereum gas fees is to use a layer 2 scaling solution. The most relevant example here is probably Loopring. In addition to being a decentralized exchange Loopring also allows you to transfer Eth and LRC to other users with zero fees. Getting your funds into Loopring does cost gas however, so whether you use this solution really depends on your end game. If you're constantly transferring Ethereum based funds to other people, Loopering is probably your best bet. You could load up your account in advance when Ethereum fees are low, and then send those assets later with no gas. Loopring could also come in handy when the time comes to sell. We all know how centralized exchanges start to experience technical issues when the price of Bitcoin or Ethereum starts to move. On Loopring you can trade wrapped Bitcoin and Ethereum for stable coins like USDC and USDT using their AMM and I doubt those trading pairs will have any outages when the market really starts to move. You also won't pay an arm and a leg in gas for a swap like you would on a layer 1 DEX like Uniswap. Just be aware, that the Loopering AMM doesn't have nearly the same volume as a centralized exchange. Meaning, you could experience some slippage with these trading pairs. To wrap things up, I want to give you a few updates about EIP1559. If you are unfamiliar Ethereum Improvement Proposal 1559 would set a base fee for Ethereum transactions and burn those fees out of circulation. The deflationary pressure of those fee burns could supercharge Ethereum's price in 2021. An Ethereum developer mentioned they would be implementing EIP1559 soon yet almost two month later it's not been done yet. This seems to be because Ethereum miners aren't exactly happy about EIP1559. To say they're making a killing from these gas fees is really an understatement and they're arguing that EIP1559 is a way of enriching speculators and investors. Given that investors like Greyscale are dying for EIP1559 to pass, I can see their point. A recent Tweet by Ethereum developer Tim Beiko suggests that they're still pressing forward with EIP1559 and that we will see it "ready to be considered for mainnet sometime in March". If I understood correctly there are only two steps left before they start testing it. I also noticed an item below the Community Outreach subheading which reads "outreach to minors to better understand their objections to 1559 and stance if it is to be deployed on mainnet". Let's just hope that's not the thing that makes or breaks this much needed upgrade to Ethereum. There's no denying that Ethereum gas fees have been too high and it seems like they're only going to get worse in the coming months. This isn't just because the network is going to get busier. It's also because there are still way too many people who don't understand how Ethereum gas works. I can't tell you the number of times I blindly set the highest transaction fee in Ethereum wallets like Metamask when sending a transaction back when I was still a crypto noob. I bet there are thousands of other Ethereum users who are needlessly doing this for every transaction, either because they're impatient or because they simply don't know any better. If everyone knew how to set the appropriate gas limit for the types of transactions they're making, maybe the gas fees would be substantially lower than they are now. While I'm a huge fan of gas tokens as a concept, I can't say I've ever used any of them in my transactions. A 50% discount on gas fees is great but if I'm still paying a few hundred Dollars for a swap after that discount, I don't see much point in using them. I also can't help but notice that the Chi gas token seems to be fairly inflated due to the speculation we're seeing as retail investors pour in. By contrast, I think there's a very good reason why layer 2s like Loopering and XDI have been performing well over the past few weeks. Even if EIP1559 is coming, the track record of Ethereum's developers suggests we're going to be waiting well past March until we see the sparks fly. Until then, layer 2s will continue to gain traction. Also don't think that Ethereum miners will actually strike down EIP1559. They're perhaps aware that if Ethereum becomes unusable, then those juicy transaction fees will disappear along with the users paying them. Moreover, Ethereum 2.0 is slowly but surely coming together. This will make proof of work mining obsolete as Ethereum 2.0 uses proof of stake mining instead. My only question is; how much longer can this go on for? Just remember to move those funds around, well before you decide to sell them and do it at a time when the network is relatively less bloated.

Chapter 8 - Lending Protocol for Crypto Loans

When I'm out hunting for small cap altcoin gems, there are a number of things that I look for. Factors that when brought together substantially increase the chance that the pick will be bang on the money. These include factors such as solving a pressing problem, being one of the first to do it, while being built in a less saturated ecosystem that has a well-supported token and one of the most promising projects that I've recently found that meets these criteria is Litentry or Lit. In order to understand Litentry, you have to appreciate the problem that it's trying to solve. Simply, it all comes down to decentralized identity management. Essentially, how do you attach unique identities to certain users on a decentralized blockchain? How do you know that a particular wallet address with which you're dealing, is controlled by a unique individual? How can you tell who that individual is? Now, I know what you're thinking; crypto is about anonymity, no one needs to know who I am. Well, that's only partly true. There are certain limits to the potential that DeFi can achieve without being able to attach identities to addresses. For example how can we deal with things like lending and credit delegation. You can borrow funds in DeFi right now but all of these loans are heavily over-collateralized. To this day, I do not know of any DeFi protocol that offers lending functionality for loans below a minimum of 140% collateralization. This is mainly for a very simple point; you don't know who you're lending to. You have no recourse if they don't pay back the loan. You can't verify their DeFi credit record. So it's only logical that you're going to ask for more collateral than they're asking for the loan. On the credit delegation point, I am not going to stand a surety for anyone else on the blockchain unless I know who they are. But that's just one of the issues that comes without identity attribution. Another one comes to decentralized governance. Currently, most proof-of-stake blockchains have a governance model where token holdings determine the weight of someone's vote. You may think that the governance mechanism is decentralized because there are a number of different wallets, however you've no way of knowing whether those wallets are controlled by a small group of individuals. This is of course a risk as we know that centralization could lead to conflicts of interest, when it comes to voting systems. This is only one of the potential issues that I foresee when one cannot adequately determine how decentralized a protocol really is. For example, what about those cases where a project wants to issue a unique airdrop to all of those individuals who've used the network? We've seen numerous examples of this in the DeFi space including Uniswap and 1 inch. This is great and all but what they've done is that they've airdropped these tokens based on unique addresses and not unique identities. So what this basically means is that if you held more than one address that used any of these protocols, you all have gotten the airdrop to more than one address. But despite whether you think that it's fair or not, it's completely within the protocol defined rules. Some may use the rules to their advantage, but if there was a way for Uniswap to have been able to identify unique users, they could have sent the airdrop to only those they knew were unique. These are only some of the benefits that come from being able to identify identities on chain, and that is exactly where Litentry comes in. Litentry is a project that's developing a platform to aggregate and manage Decentralized Identifiers or DIDs across numerous different blockchains. Basically a platform for projects and protocols to manage and use DIDs as an input into new and exciting features. More importantly, Litentry is trying to build a protocol that will allow these DIDs to be used privately and securely. When it comes to the underlying network, Litentry is built on Substrate. Substrate is a framework for building decentralized blockchains. Highly efficient and easy to build on. However one of the most exciting things about building on Substrate is that it is natively compatible with Polkadot. That means that it could eventually be launched as a Parachain on the Polkadot network. The benefits of this are immense. Ethereum is going through some severe scaling issues currently and until Ethereum 2.0 is launched, things are unlikely to improve much.

Polkadot will be much more scalable than Ethereum, given the unique nature of its consensus mechanism. Moreover, through this unique Parachain architecture it means that DAPps built on Polkadot Parachains are interoperable. They can be used across a number of other blockchains and ecosystems. There is of course a lot more to Polkadot than this. What's important to know is what this means for Litentry. It means that it can be used for cross-chain identity management. It does not have to be restricted to merely the Polkadot ecosystem. This means that DAPps that are built on Ethereum. Cosmos or Filecoin can make use of the did system developed by Litentry. DAPps like Compound, Uniswap and AAve could use Litentry crosschain identity services to expand their product lines. For example, there are credit delegation in AAve too. This basically would mean that someone could backstop the credit for someone else on the

AAve platform. Though given that there is no way of confirming the identity and credit record of these users natively, they had to outsource this to the open law smart contracts. That being said if they were able to use a service like Litentry, this could be done seamlessly and on chain. They would be able to immediately verify the decentralized credit record of the counterparty in a private and secure way. Litentry sounds exciting, but how does it work? Let's take a high level look at the Litentry architecture. Firstly let's take a look at the user side technology and the primary piece of technology here is the Litentry mobile app. The app will be integrated with the latency network and will allow users to participate in the governance process and access identity-based services. The app could also be linked to other networks and even some traditional identity verification systems like LinkedIn. They will also be able to manage lit incentives here and also use it as a crypto wallet. The app will include the Litentry authenticator. This is the mobile identity and data hub for the web 3.0 ecosystem. You can actually get a sense of how this looks over on the initial proposal of the app over in their docs. They also have a github repo dedicated to the app that you can view as well. What's pretty neat is that you can actually also try out some features on late entry right now over with their DAPp playground. This is basically a hub of decentralized web applications built on Litentry. It demonstrates how the two-factor authentication will work. You can use it with no passwords or registration just to get a sense of how the tech will function. That's the user side features, however the real hardcore tech that's been developed is over on the developer side. Firstly, you have the core Litentry network. This is built on Substrate and hence uses one of the most well-known frameworks out there. A framework that includes some of the most robust and efficient byzantine consensus mechanisms. On a more technical level, the Litentry runtime protocol will be able to link an account across all other chains, using that unique identifier. The users on Litentry can sign transactions attached to their unique identity with a private key. The benefits of this are that the user data can be shared but privately. Nothing about the user themselves apart from the unique identifier is actually shared. This identifier can also be linked to on-chain crypto assets to verify information relevant for credit delegation. The exact mechanics of how Litentry network works is beyond the scope of this book. The most important thing to take away from this substrate architecture is the ability to easily upgrade to become a Parachain on the Polkadot ecosystem. Something else that Litentry is building in their tech stack is an SDK or Software Development Kit. This will be essential in order to encourage developers to build client-side applications on top of Litentry network. These currently support Javascript which is one of the most popular programming language out there, so that would ease developer adoption on the network. I should also note that in Litentry whitepaper they say that they're planning to add more language support to these SDKs, and one final piece of the latency architecture is their Light Client Services. These basically enable the Litentry mobile applications to be independent of third-party servers. More technically, it means that these apps can connect directly to the Litentry blockchain without having to rely on any single node. This of course has benefits when it comes to trust and decentralization. It prevents any situation where malicious nodes can feed false information to the clients. That's a bit of an overview of the Litentry architecture. Something that is no doubt central to the Litentry network and ecosystem is that Lit token. Lit is the native utility token on the Litentry network and performs a number of different functions. Firstly, it's used to pay for fees. There are a number of different fees that users will have to pay on the network. These include fees such as transaction fees to prevent spamming of the network, matching fees which are paid by applications to identity stakers; this incentivizes more people to stake identities on the network, validation fees paid to what are termed identity guardians who take responsibility for validating staking identities and ordering the data into an acceptable format. So, that's the utility generated from fees on the network, but Lit tokens are also used for staking purposes. Identity registrars are third parties that can set up indexed identity databases. These databases are then queried for the decentralized identifiers. In order to make sure that these registrars have skin in the game, they have monetary incentives and disincentives. This means that if there's any dishonest behaviour, they will have their stakes slashed or lost. Of course, they'll also earn rewards from providing these identity services. These block rewards for the stakers are paid in Lit. I should also note that because Lit will have economic value within a DeFi ecosystem. It can also be used as collateral. For example, if someone with an identity verifier on the lit entry network wants to lend some crypto, then they can deposit Lit as the collateral, so that's another form of utility right there. And of course, as is the case with most DeFi protocols, Lit will also be used in the decentralized governance of the protocol. It will determine the voting power of the individuals on the network. This could be decisions like functionality to add to the network or whether to remove any dishonest guardians. One more use case that they'll be for, Lit tokens is to be a grant that the team allocates two developers that build on Litentry, so as an incentive mechanism. Given that these developers have been rewarded an economic piece of the network, they will earn those rewards. Litentry has developed quite a lot of use cases for their token. I've not seen many projects at this stage of development that have structured such a comprehensive ecosystem for their tokens, but in order to understand its long-term potential, we have to take a look at the tokenomics. Firstly, let's start off with the initial distribution of the tokens. There is a total supply of 100 million Lit. These tokens were split according to the following; 15% to the Litentry team, 8% went to the seed investors, 12% to private sale and further sales, 17% will be reserved for the foundation to be used as grants, 3% to Binance launch pool and a full 45% to remain as network incentives in the Parachain auction system. When it comes to initial distribution, I think this is reasonably fair. If we include the founder allocation into the broader network incentives bucket, including launch pool, it's a full 65% that will eventually be released to the community. What's important though from an investment perspective is to determine potential supply headwinds from token unlock schedules. Users are no doubt concerned about the potential for initial sales to be dumped on the market. Well, the initial release is reasonable with steady unlock periods every quarter. In other words, there are no large release cliffs which could flood the markets with supply. The 3% released during the Binance launch pool has already been distributed and are in circulating supply. The Parachain auctions and block reward inflation will only start in November of 2025. Once the block rewards start, the rate of inflation will be determined by the amount that's staked on the network. The target network participation rate is 70% which would imply a 5% inflation rate. This is actually quite mild for a proof-of-stake blockchain. So from a supply perspective, Lit is unlikely to face either supply saturation or extensive inflation. All positive for long-term price appreciation. Of course, we also cannot forget that price is a function of supply and demand, and demand is likely to be quite strong for Lid. What makes me think this? Well, firstly from a protocol design perspective, the more the network is used, the more utility demand there will be for the token. The more demand there is to stake identities to pay for computations and to be used as collateral for lending services. There are no projects that currently provide similar services to Litentry, so when they do eventually launch there will be extensive demand for these decentralized identity services in the DeFi space. It's only logical. Then we also have to consider investment demand. Lit has already crossed a major hurdle by being listed on tier one exchange. Since Lit came out, the launch pool and the token began trading. The volume took off like crazy along with the price. There was a lot of demand to hodl' Lit and I think that this is likely to gain momentum. This is due to a number of factors. Firstly you have to consider that it's a project that will be launched as a Parachain on Polkadot. You only need to take a look at some of the excitement around Polkadot-based projects to get a sense of how much untapped demand there is here. There is a growing sense that DeFi tokens based on Polkadot could see similar price appreciation to those we saw in the Ethereum ecosystem back in 2020. As long as the market believes that, price momentum is likely to pick up. Finally, is also important to point out the fact that Litentry has its roots in Asia. For example the team is from China and most of the VC backers are from countries such as China and Vietnam. Investors in these regions tend to be more blockchain and crypto crazy than those in the west. This means that once Litentry is launched, there could be an immense frenzy from buyers in this region to pick up the tokens. What really drew me to Litentry was the problem that they're solving in the DeFi space. I had not seen or heard about a project that was offering similar identity-based verifications in any ecosystem. Being able to verify the unique identity of wallet addresses, is the missing key to DeFi offering many of the other services that centralized finance relies on. Under collateralized lending and credit delegation are features that are just not on the DeFi menu yet.

Not until we can verify identities and even then, DeFi currently lacks the mechanisms to fully identify how decentralized their networks are. All of these problems can be solved with Litentry's technology. Moreover, given that it could be upgraded to a Polkadot Parachain, this means that it will be built on one of the most exciting ecosystems in the crypto space right now. Scalable, interoperable and highly functional. Something else I really liked about the Litentry team is how much work has been done on the idea already. Unlike many other early stage projects that try to raise millions on nothing more than a white paper, these guys have already built numerous concepts and pushed hundreds of lines of code. All completely free to explore in their github repos. I should also note that Litentry has a really exciting roadmap, both for their runtime development and their mobile application, so there's a lot to look forward to on the tech front over the coming months. Apart from that, I like the tokenomics of Lit. It seems that they've attempted to cover all bases and create real utility value for the token. Add to that the fact that supply growth is relatively mild and there is a reasonable token unlock schedule. Of course it also helps that there's a great deal of demand to hodl' Lit. There is a strong community that has already rallied behind it and as we know community engagement helps to drive buzz around the project. Are there risks? Well, there always are. There is a risk that the project does not launch on a Parachain, and a competing protocol may do it better. There is a risk of a security breach in the future that could expose personal info on chain. But these risks are known and have been incorporated into my risk-reward analysis. Remember, you will have to decide if it fits your personal risk profile.

Chapter 9 - The Comprehensive Binance Trading Guide

Have you found that legendary altcoin and need to branch out from the likes of Coinbase to get it? If you're nodding along to any of that, then you're probably going to want an exchange that gives you access to hundreds of altcoins and trading pairs. One that gives you multiple options to deposit Dollars, Pounds, Euros, or maybe you're even interested in having the option to trade futures, earn interest on your crypto, get a crypto visa card or take part in one of those mysterious IEOs like the one your friend made a lots of money? Well, the good news is that there is an exchange that offers all that and more. That would be the number one crypto exchange in the World; Binance. So in this chapter I'll explain you exactly how to buy Bitcoin with that regular fiat currency, I'll walk you through how to trade on the exchange and I'll provide you with a complete overview of Binance's other major features. To kick things off I'm going to have to start with a bit of an overview of Binance as a company. After all, it's probably a good idea to know who you're dealing with before depositing any money on a platform. No one really knows where Binance is headquartered. You'll have many people saying Malta, however about a year ago the Maltese regulator came out to say that Binance isn't under Maltese jurisdiction. Some people like to make a big deal of that, but do you really need to ask yourself where Bitcoin is headquartered? I guess that's the problem with businesses in crypto like Binance and it's maybe best not to judge them like you would a traditional company. Binance is global and has lots of offices around the World with staff in around 50 countries. The guys at Binance are also not exactly hiding. Indeed, the opposite is true. You have Binance's legendary founder Changpeng Zhao or CZ making waves and taking names in interviews, Twitter and even appearing on the front cover of Forbes magazine. Speaking of Forbes, according to the bean counters over there CZ turns out to be the fifth wealthiest person in crypto with a net worth estimated at a staggering 1.9 billion Dollars. Binance exchange launched back in 2017 after a successful ICO that raised 15 million Dollars. Those investors got BNB coins in return for an initial value of around 10 cents. Flash forward today and BNB is worth over 100 Dollars. Not a bad return for those who had faith in CZ from the get-go. In 2019 you had Binance reporting profits of around 570 million Dollars with CZ announcing at the end of 2020 that the exchange expected to record about 1 billion Dollars in profits for the year. Those crazy profits are thanks to Binance processing around 2 billion in trades a day on average. But Binance doesn't stop there. The exchange actually has a much bigger stake in the crypto ecosystem than Binance alone. Last year it acquired the crypto card provider called Swipe, a project valued at around 200 million Dollars. Binance also acquired coinmarketcap.com for a reported 400 million Dollars and the popular crypto storage solution Trust wallet back in 2018. Other strategic investments include the likes of FTX exchange whose token is a top 40 crypto in its own right and is valued at around 2 billion Dollars market cap. This is by no means an extensive list of everything that Binance has strategically invested in or required. But I think you get the point. The Binance exchange isn't exactly a backstreet exchange run out of some basement. Instead, you have the most successful crypto exchange on the planet led by a founder who's achieved in three and a half years what would take most billionaires a lifetime. To top that all off, Binance has invested a pretty penny in further widening its footprint in the wider ecosystem. Put very simply, if there were any shenanigans going on at Binance, they have a heck of a lot to lose. Also Binance has a track record of doing the right thing too. They got hacked in 2019 where around two percent of the Bitcoin holdings on the exchange were lost, however Binance fully reimbursed everyone impacted by that hack by tapping funds from the Safu fund which is a pot of crypto put aside to cover things like exchange hacks. Binance is a really big deal in the crypto World and they have a track record for ensuring that their users are taken care of. All major reasons why I am personally happy to use Binance as my primary crypto exchange. Now that you have that overview,

I want to move on and explain how to find out if that hot altcoin you want is actually listed on the exchange. After all, there's not much point in getting an account good to go if it aren't there. This little trick will show you every exchange that a specific cryptocurrency can be traded on. To do that you can hop on over to coinmarketcap.com, click the search function and type in the crypto you're looking for. Once you've clicked on the crypto, you will see a stats page with a bunch of different metrics and a price chart. If you look above the price chart, you'll see a bunch of different options and one of those will be a market button. Click little guy and you'll see all the different exchanges that crypto is listed on, along with the different trading pairs available. For example you might see that AVAX can be bought on Binance with USDC, BTC Turkish lira, BUSD and BNB coin. Also, another thing to know is that Binance typically has the highest trading volume for pretty much every cryptocurrency that it supports. So most people trading the coin in question are doing so on Binance. You can replicate that method for any cryptocurrency to find out where you can get it. The truth is that signing up to Binance is really simple so I'm not going to bore you with a step-by-step guide on how to do that. I trust you'll use a really strong password though for your account. Once you've set up your Binance account, make sure you set up two-factor authentication using Google authenticator. That is important for security. However I do want to move on now and explain how to deposit fiat currency; Dollars and Euros on Binance. Once you've created your Binance account, secured it with a really strong password and two-factor authentication, you are ready to get down to business and make a deposit. What makes Binance a great exchange to get into crypto is that there are just so many options. If you click the buy crypto button at the top of the home page, you'll see a currency symbol. Once you've clicked on that, it will show you a drop down of all the different fiat currencies you can deposit. There are literally dozens of different currencies to choose from. The payment options will change according to which currency you select. Binance offers the greatest selection of currencies with which you can buy crypto. What's really cool with Binance is that some of these deposit methods are zero fee so you'll basically be getting the most bang for your buck. If you're living in the UK, chances are you're going to want to use that zero fee bank deposit to get those Pounds onto Binance. If you are based in Europe, Sepa deposits are free. You can also get Australian deposits fee free by using Pay ID or Osco. I do need to say that not every country will have fee-free deposit options, so just be aware of that. Also those tempted just to use their bank card to make that deposit on Binance, should maybe think again. It's convenient however those Visa or Mastercard deposits will be charged at 1.8% for Euros or GBP and at 3.1% for Rubles. If you're in one of those countries where the only option is high card fees on Binance, you may want to use a local exchange with lower fiat on-ramp fees. You can then send Bitcoin from this exchange to Binance in order to buy that hot altcoin you crave. Another important thing to note is that although Binance supports a ton of different currencies but it certainly doesn't support every currency in the World. So, if your native currency isn't supported, you're probably going to want to deposit US Dollars. Once you click select a deposit method, you'll be taken to the deposit page. If you selected a bank deposit, you'll then see two options. You can deposit by bank card and pay that 1.8% fee which is literally as simple as keying in the amount you want to deposit, clicking continue, enter in your card details and smashing that pay button. Or, you can use the free bank deposit option. In the UK, you can use something known as faster payments. The slight annoyance with this option is that you'll have to enter some additional ID information. It is however as simple as digging out your passport entering that passport id and selecting your country. Once done, you'll then see some bank details to use to make your deposit. You can just hop on into your online banking and make that transfer. What's really important to note though, is that you must use the same payment reference for that transaction that you see in Binance. That way, Binance knows that it's your deposit and that it should be assigned to your account. Once your deposit has gone through and you have those Pounds or Euros in your Binance account, you want to go to the buy crypto tab again and select cash balance from the drop down. You'll then see the page where you can enter how much and which crypto you want to buy and click that buy button. Before you make that purchase, you can also see how much cryptocurrency you'll be getting too. That is basically all there is to it if you want to deposit on Binance. But what if you have some crypto already and want to partake in that altcoin buffet on the exchange? Well, to deposit crypto on Binance, you'll want to log into your account and click the wallet button at the top left of the screen. This will expand a drop down and you'll see something called fiat and spot. Click that. You'll then be taken to the screen where you want to click that deposit button. You'll then see a deposit page for Bitcoin with a BTC address. If you want to deposit BTC, then just use that address to send your Bitcoin to Binance, however if you have an altcoin you want to deposit instead, you can just click that Bitcoin button to expand a drop down and search for the crypto you want to deposit on Binance. Then you can generate a deposit address to use to ship that crypto over to Binance to trade. Now you have the overview of how to deposit funds on Binance. I now want to move on and tell you how you can optimize those trading fees. I also have a few tips on where you can find Binance promotions to take advantage of. Fees might sound boring but trust me they add up and can cost you lots over the long term. Firstly, you need to know that there are two types of trading fees in crypto. The first is the taker fee which is when you execute an order at the current market price. Secondly, you have what is known as a maker fee, which you pay when you provide liquidity by placing things like a limit order. I would bet that the vast majority of people new to crypto will be paying taker fees so let's focus on that for now. Taker and maker fee start at just 0.1%. To put that into context, Coinbase pro charges a five times higher default taker fee at 0.5%. There are several ways to further reduce those finance fees. The first is by trading more than 50 Bitcoin in 30 days. That's a heck of a lot of trading volume. Or, alternatively you can hold more than 50 BNB in your account to get that slightly reduced maker fee. 50BNB is worth over 5,000. If you want to discount on those taker fees, you'll have to trade a mere 4,500 BTC in 30 days or hold 1000 BNB. That's over 100k in BNB coin. Who's got that money lying around? Well, trying to reduce those trading fees by trading volumes or holding BNB alone is sub-optimal. Instead I like to always hold a bit of BNB in my account and use that to pay for my trading fees. Do that and you'll automatically get 25% off those fees and will be paying just 0.075 percent. Another thing that I see many people ignoring are the fantastic promotions on Binance. Most of these promotions are geared towards crypto trading junkies, but it is still worth your while to scroll through and see if you can get value from any of them. For example, if you were looking to trade Reef, there was a $50,000 trading competition on. Despite the fact that the lion's share goes to those hardcore traders, there is often a lottery element to the promotion. In this Reef trading competition, 20 lucky people who had traded Reef were chosen at random to get 500 Dollars in Reef tokens each. Now you know how to reduce those trading fees and make use of those promotions. But I'm sure that you're itching to start trading altcoins on Binance so let's see how it's done. There are several ways to trade on Binance.

Let's start by looking at the easiest way. Firstly you'll want to make sure you're logged into your Binance account, then click trade from the top menu bar and select convert from the drop-down. You'll then be taken to the screen where you can select the cryptos you want to convert and select the amount you want to swap. You might want to swap 100 BNB to BUSD. You just enter that in, and bash preview conversion. You'll see a quoted price and you have a few seconds to accept that price. Once done, your trade is complete. It's literally as easy as that. The downside to this method is that there are only a limited number of trading pairs and it only supports market orders, which means you have to take the current market price. Personally, I prefer more flexibility and you can get that in the classic trading panel. You can hop on over there by selecting trade from the top navigation bar and choosing classic from the drop down.

If that looks complicated, take a step back and don't panic. I promise you it's not as complicated as it might first appear. The value in this type of trading interface is that it can allow you to place more advanced order types, which can end up saving you a lot more money and save you a load of time into the bargain. To explain what's going on with this trading interface, we should look at it in sections. To the left, you have the order book. All those red numbers at the top are orders to sell a particular cryptocurrency and all the green ones are orders to buy. All those orders are made at different prices. The left-hand column in the order book is the price that people have placed buy or sell orders at. The middle column is the amount of crypto available at certain price points, and finally we have the right hand column in the order book which displays the Dollar value available at different price points. In the center of the screen you can see a price graph. You can filter that according to different time periods. Also you can click the little yellow tab to bring up charting tools. This is if you would like to perform technical analysis. On the top right of the trading panel, you have all the different trading pairs available on Binance. You can use that search function to find the cryptocurrency you're looking to trade. Once you have searched for your crypto, you can see all the different trading pairs come up. You probably have two questions; the first is what on earth do those 5x and 3x symbols mean next to some of those trading pairs? Well, these just mean that you can trade on five times or three times leverage via margin trading. That's where you borrow funds to trade on leverage and amplify gains and losses. If you're just starting off I would seriously recommend ignoring leverage until you are an experienced trader and fully understand the risks. Also just remember that trading pairs use abbreviated versions of the cryptocurrencies, called tickers. This is usually a combination of three or four letters. But how do you find the ticker for the crypto you want to get? Well, you can hop on over to Coinmarketcap and search for the crypto that you're interested in. The ticker will display to the right of the cryptocurrency's name. You can use that method to find the ticker for any crypto. Back to that trading panel, at the bottom right corner you have market trades. This just shows the most recent trades that have been executed, and finally you have the section of the trading panel where all the magic happens and where you place those all-important orders.

By default, this order menu will be set to limit orders. The best way of explaining what these are is to use an example. So let's say I don't like the current

Bitcoin price but I'm a happy buyer at 40,000 Dollars. I can actually place that order on Binance by typing in that 40K price point and choosing the amount of Bitcoin I want to buy. If I do that and place that limit order by smashing the buy Bitcoin button, that order will then be added to the order book. If I'm asleep and the BTC price plunges to 40K on Binance, then this limit order should automatically trigger and I'll get my Bitcoin at this lower price. So this is why you might want to use limit orders rather than those market orders. What's also important to note is that limit orders attract maker and not taker fees, which can sometimes be cheaper on Binance. Limit orders work exactly the same on the sell side. I might put a limit order in for one Bitcoin if the price reaches 100K. That order will just sit there and do nothing until the price point is hit. Of course these orders are always cancellable. You can also set the order to be live for only a certain period of time. Market orders are the simplest types of orders. You're simply entering an amount you want to buy and taking the current market price. By now you should know the basics on how to buy and sell crypto using market and limit orders. One thing I did want to bring your attention to is the futures tab. You're probably going to want to avoid that. It's even riskier than mere margin trading. Futures can be a useful tool if used responsibly by professional traders. But newbies trading volatile altcoins with 125 times leverage is not a responsible use of them. If you insist on trading with leverage, then you could consider leveraged tokens. These give you moderate leverage but eliminate the risk of getting liquidated, so a decent compromise. That's the basic trading functionality over on Binance, however this is just one of the plethora of services offered on crypto. So let's take a look at what else is on the menu. With all this global money printing going on, I'm sure you are getting pretty poultry rates of interest on your funds. Well, Binance Earn gives you the option to earn interest rates of around 6% APY on some crypto currencies. You can choose to opt for flexible savings which means you can access your crypto at any time. Or you can lock that crypto in for terms of up to 90 days for a slightly higher interest rate. High risk savings products are available for even higher rates. But just be aware that you're taking on more risk to get that yield. The reason why these interest generating products are so popular, is that many people hodl crypto in a wallet and it sits there doing nothing. Some people take a portion of their holdings to earn interest while they're waiting for those crypto prices to explode to levels that they're happy with. Another hot product Binance offers is their crypto Visa card.

Why on earth would you want one? Well, let's face it, converting crypto and withdrawing that money to your bank can be a hassle. Also, if you've ever experienced 20% gains in a day? I can tell you first-hand that you're likely going to want to go out and treat yourself to a little something. If that interests you and you want to be able to spend your crypto wherever Visa is accepted, then a crypto card is what you need. The good news for anyone living in most European countries is that you can get your hands on a sweet Binance card. That Binance black card is completely free and Binance themselves don't charge you any admin or processing fees. That card also links with your Binance exchange account which is pretty awesome too. Even better, you can get up to 8% cashback when you use that card. So if you're lucky enough to be able to get a Binance card, then you might want to grab one. I don't really recommend people do this but Binance also offers collateralized crypto loans too. The way to think about this is that it's a bit like getting a loan at a pawn broker where you supply collateral in the form of an item with value like a watch and you get cash lent against it. On Binance you can get an initial loan to value ratio of 55% and you'll be asked to add more crypto to secure your loan if the LTV rises to 75%. If that LTV gets to 83%, your crypto collateral will be sold by Binance to cover the loan, which is something you certainly don't want to happen. What most people do with these loans is to buy more crypto which is a form of leveraging. But if you are into that you can supply crypto collateral and even be lent Euros, Pounds or US Dollars if you want. Then you have a feature known as the Binance Liquid Swap. That's another way you can generate passive income with crypto and potentially earn high yield, but be warned, it comes with risks. Next you have something known as the Launch Pool. Basically this product allows finance users to acquire new token rewards in return for staking certain cryptocurrencies. Some cryptos like Lit didn't have a public sale or initial exchange offering at all and instead distributed a portion of the initial token using the Launch Pool. The last product is the Binance Launch Pad. This is Binance's exclusive launch platform for crypto projects. It's also where people can get token allocations at highly favorable prices. For popular Launchpad projects, the token allocations are typically done via a lottery system. Put simply, the more BNB coins you hold in your Binance account, the more lottery tickets you get. Win the lottery, and you get the right to buy a specific altcoin at a set price. Each winning lottery ticket for the injective public sale on Binance launch pad entitled the winner to buy 200 Dollars' worth of INJ at 40 cents a token. In around four months, those INJ tokens reached around 15 Dollars a token. A pretty incredible return for anyone who got involved in that one. Provided you pick a solid project and are lucky enough to get an allocation, the chances are that you'll do pretty well as soon as public trading goes live on Binance. That's the reason why pretty much every project that's ever been launched on Launchpad has been chronically oversubscribed and why that lottery system was implemented. It was Binance's attempt to make these allocations more equitable and fair. Also, it isn't as if Binance shares these initial exchange offerings with other exchanges. So, if you see a project on the launch pad, that opportunity will be exclusive to Binance. It's well worth hitting that launch pad out to see if anything tickles. Finally, I do want to take a few moments out to talk about some of the educational resources that Binance offers for free. The first would be Binance Academy, which provides some great overviews on different cryptos and cryptocurrency related topics. I would certainly recommend checking that out. Another thing that I think is really underappreciated is Binance research. Here you can find project reports with all manner of stats and graphics, covering things like a project's token supply, token allocation, release schedule and more. All that is presented in a really digestible form. I think you will find these research reports quite helpful when conducting your own research. That about wraps up my beginner's guide to Binance. The truth is that I've just scratched the surface on what Binance offers. There is a whole lot more but you should really start using Binance and see which options are most interested to you.

Chapter 10 - FTX, Huobi & BNB Tokens for Trading

If you've been watching the cryptocurrency leader boards closely then you've probably noticed an interesting phenomenon. Exchange tokens are quickly rising up the ranks and almost all of them have seen exponential growth over the past few months. This is not all that surprising given that these tokens offer perks to traders on their respective exchanges and trading volumes on centralized exchanges have increased in accordance with the bull market. But that's not all these exchange tokens are used for. Many cryptocurrency exchanges are also building out their own centralized DeFi ecosystems, which add an entirely new dimension of use cases to exchange tokens, namely as payment for network fees. If Binance's BNB is any indication, these exchange tokens may just be getting started. So in this chapter I'm going to be taking a closer look at the Binance coin as well as the Huobi token and the FTX token to see if they have any actual potential or whether all this recent price action is just smoke and mirrors. Binance is the largest cryptocurrency exchange in the World by trading volume it was founded in China and moved out of the country in 2017 prior to the Chinese government's ban on crypto trading. While Binance is based in Malta it is technically registered in the Cayman Islands and Seychelles. BNB is a cryptocurrency used in Binance's ecosystem. Given the size of this ecosystem, BNB has no shortage of use cases. For starters, over 90 percent of Binance employees receive their salary in BNB. On the Binance exchange, traders can get a 25% discount on trading fees when paying them in BNB, and according to the BNB white paper this trading discount will diminish as time goes on and BNB will no longer provide any perks for traders after July 2022. There are over 100 trading pairs with BNB on the Binance exchange with ample volume. BNB can also be used for everyday purchases via the Binance Card and will be one of the five cryptocurrencies supported by the upcoming Binance pay service. Binance pay is described as a "crypto based paypal rival" and is expected to launch in alpha sometime next year. That said, BNB can already be used to book flights and hotels, buy music and gift cards and even pay for website servers. Merchants can also accept BNB as payment using over half a dozen plugins including "Coin payments" and "Now payments". Yet it seems most of the demand for BNB is coming from its use in Binance's booming cDeFi ecosystem, where it's used for trading collateral for lending liquidity mining and of course gas fees. BNB initially began as an ERC20 token and sold during an ICO round held by Binance in the summer of 2017. This saw 100 million BNB sold at a cost of around 11 cents each, raising around 15 million Dollars in total. 80 million BNB were allocated to the Binance team and another 20 million BNB were given to angel investors. BNB had initial supply of 200 million and is deflationary due to the quarterly burns conducted by Binance. This is where Binance uses 20% of its quarterly profits to burn BNB. This burning will continue until the supply of BNB reaches 100 million. So far just under 30 million BNB has been burned with the most recent burn taking place in January 2021. Binance CEO CZ noted that he wants to accelerate the burning of BNB so that the 100 million target is met within the next five to eight years. It is worth pointing out that this is not entirely clear where these burned tokens are coming from. References to Binance's "repurchasing plans were removed from the Binance white paper in April 2019". To add to the confusion, Binance announced that same month that they would be burning the 80 million BNB team allocation as part of their on-going quarterly burns, instead of investing it over four years. Binance apparently holds just over 53 million BNB between four wallets on the Binance chain, which is now the native chain of the BNB coin. This 27 million BNB difference lines up quite nicely with the amount of BNB burned so far. In addition to the Binance chain, BNB also exists on the Binance smart chain as a BEP20 token, where it's used to pay for gas fees to interact with various cDeFi protocols. The total value locked in these cDeFi protocols corresponds quite nicely to the price action of BNB, which has seen a comfortable 5x since the start of the 2021. BNB is the largest of all exchange tokens and by a comfortable margin. While it may continue to grow, this growth seems to depend on Binance's cDeFi ecosystem and the adoption of those protocols seems to boil down to the low gas fees offered by the Binance smart chain. Low gas fees are the only selling point of Binance's cDeFi ecosystem. There does not seem to be very much originality or innovation going on in that space. Most of the protocols are just carbon copies of popular Ethereum DeFi protocols, which is where most of the DeFi innovation continues to happen, despite those high gas costs. That said, Ethereum is apparently weeks away from passing EIP1559, which would essentially solve all the issues relating to gas fees and send the price of Eth to the moon. When EIP1559 is implemented, there would not be much reason for DeFi Degen to stay on the Binance smart chain. But until that day comes, BNB will continue to grow.

Moving onto the Huobi token, it is the second largest cryptocurrency exchange by trading volume. It was founded in China in 2013 and is registered in Seychelles. In contrast to Binance, Huobi opted to change its business model in response to the 2017 ban by the Chinese government. Huobi China now operates as a consulting company which focuses on blockchain technologies. Huobi group owns multiple cryptocurrency exchanges Worldwide including Huobi global, Huobi career and the soon to be reinstated Huobi US. Huobi is also a publicly traded company on the Hong Kong Stock Exchange and Huobi CEO Leon Lee is apparently on very good terms with the Chinese government. The Huobi token is a cryptocurrency used in Huobi's ecosystem. On Huobi cryptocurrency exchanges, just holding the Huobi token in your exchange wallet, can give you a trading fee discount of up to 65% It also lets you access exclusive token sales and lets you earn rewards on special occasions in the cryptocurrency space, like Bitcoin pizza day. Like BNB, the Huobi token can be used to pay for services from various merchants, though the list is not nearly as extensive. Unlike BNB, holding the Huobi token lets you vote on any proposed changes to the cryptocurrency exchange. While Huobi has been working on a smart contract blockchain called the Huobi chain since 2019 with Nervous network, the Huobi chain has yet to exit its test net phase. In contrast to Binance's cDeFi and DeFi in general, the Huobi chain is meant to be compliant with Chinese regulations and will require KYC to use. According to a Decrypt article, the Huobi chain's key feature is quote that it allows the Chinese government to have a regulator node that will give the government unbridled access to all on-chain data. To say that not many people will be comfortable with that is something of an understatement. Still, Chinese investors are hungry for DeFi and giving them access to a compliant way to be DeFi Degen, is certainly worth a lot of money. Still, it's questionable if the Huobi token will play a role in Huobi's DeFi ecosystem. This is because the Huobi token is an ERC20 token that was sold in a way which probably doesn't sit well with regulators. Instead of an ICO, Huobi used a points card system in February 2018. Exchange users were able to purchase points cards which would make them eligible to receive "free Huobi tokens". The details are a bit complicated but these points card sales worked out to an average price of around $1.50 per Huobi token. 300 million Huobi tokens were given away for free, and Huobi apparently raised 300 million Dollars from their points card sales. The Huobi token has a maximum supply of 500 million. Of the remaining 200 million Huobi tokens, 100 million were reserved for future incentives, and 100 million were allocated to the Huobi team with a four-year vesting schedule. Like Binance and BNB, Huobi allocates 20% of its revenue to burning Huobi tokens. Unlike Binance, Huobi specifies that 15% of this revenue is used to purchase and burn tokens from the circulating supply and the remaining 5% is used to burn Huobi tokens allocated to the team. This means that Huobi's token burns likely have a greater impact on the price than Binances with BNB. Huobi bought and burned Huobi tokens on a quarterly basis until 2020, when they switched to burning on a monthly basis. Huobi has burned 250 million Huobi tokens so far and as this burning is set to continue until all Huobi tokens have been burned. The Huobi token is the second largest exchange token by market cap. When it comes to price action, it has performed almost as well as BNB since the start of the year. This is actually quite bizarre given that the Huobi token does not have nearly as much market demand as BNB. It is possible that this price action is almost entirely due to Huobi's buying and burning of Huobi tokens. This behavior basically guarantees an appreciation in price for the Huobi token. But I wonder how long this gravy train is going to stay on the rails. Despite the CEO's strong connections to Chinese authorities, Huobi seems to have come under serious regulatory scrutiny over the last few months. Two of the exchange's top-ranking executives were arrested in November and December due to suspicions that Huobi's OTC trading services were used to launder money. According to a recent Coindesk article the case is also "politically sensitive". While this likely won't have any impact on Huobi group's cryptocurrency exchanges around the World, it might put a wrench in Huobi's plans to roll out a compliant DeFi ecosystem in China. Any negative news about Huobi would also put a dent in the price of the Huobi token as it did in the fall and something tells me that Huobi's OTC investigation is going to make a few more painful headlines before it's resolved. By contrast, I've only seen good things about the FTX exchange in the news. FTX is a cryptocurrency derivatives exchange that is "built by traders for traders". Derivatives are just instruments that get their value from other assets. Derivatives include the likes of options and futures etc. FTX was incubated in 2019 by Alameda Research a cryptocurrency trading firm founded by former wall street trader Sam Bankman-Freed. Sam is the CEO of the FTX exchange and is also known for being very active in the cryptocurrency community. Like the other crypto exchanges covered so far, FTX is registered in the Caribbean specifically Antigua and Barbuda. FTX is currently the fourth largest derivatives exchange by trading volume. Even though it processes only a fraction of the volume of Binance and Huobis features platforms, FTX features more than seven times the amount of tradable assets. Many of FTX's futures markets are unique and let you do things like trade stocks before they IPO and profit when altcoins drop using FTX's Index token. FTX's FTT token can be used as collateral when trading these futures contracts. While FTX has no native DeFi ecosystem FTT token holders were airdropped SRM to motivate them to use the serum DEX which is built on the Solana blockchain. Holding FTT can also give discounts on trading fees of up to 60% and even gives a cut of any excess capital in FTX's insurance fund to FTT holders. This insurance fund exists to minimize clawbacks. A clawback is when traders who are in profit, must give back some of those profits to ensure the exchange remains solvent during times of high market volatility. These are just a few of the benefits bestowed by the FTT token. FTT is an ERC20 token. Although there was no ICO for it, just over 73 million FTT was sold to private investors in three rounds with price tags ranging from 10 cents to 80 cents per FTT. These sales rated in roughly 10 million Dollars and accounted for just under 20% of FTT's initial supply of 350 million. 175 million FTT were allocated to FTX with a three-year vesting schedule and the remaining 100 or so million FTT went to various initiatives on the FTX platform such as liquidity for FTT trading pairs. Some of these remaining FTT tokens also apparently went to the FTX team and company. That's apparently in addition to the 175 million. This skewed allocation really doesn't matter however, because FTT has a more aggressive buyback and burn schedule than any other exchange token on the crypto market. 33% of all trading fees on FTX go towards weekly buybacks and burns of the FTT token. This is in addition to the 10% of additions to the insurance fund and 5% of all other fees on FTX. 10 million FTT have been burned so far, which is pretty impressive when you consider how new FTX is compared to other crypto exchanges. On that note, FTT is one of the only exchange tokens with ample liquidity on other reputable exchanges, namely Binance which purchased a stake in FTX in December 2019. Although the Dollar amount of this investment was not disclosed, it's possible it involved the purchase of the 10 million FTT we now see on the Binance chain. The fact the FTT token has ample volume on other exchanges, increases the likelihood that the price is not being manipulated by FTX, which seems to be the case for many other exchange tokens. When it comes to price, FTT has seen a 3x since the start of 2021 and currently sits as the third largest exchange token by market cap. Given that it's currently ranked 40th by market cap overall, it still has a lot of room to grow and so does the FTX exchange for that matter. The only problem is that not everyone trades derivatives and futures. Amateur traders coming into the crypto market also have enough of a learning curve already. FTX has done a good job of putting themselves in the news. This is thanks to the innovative new products and markets they create on an almost weekly basis. Many of these markets are enticing traders on other exchanges to pay a visit to FTX. Most importantly, the FTT token has some serious utility that's not reliant on Ethereum, having high gas fees or price manipulation by the exchanges which issued it. For these reasons I think FTT is the best of the three exchange tokens I've covered in this chapter. There are other exchange tokens too but many aren't even worth considering and some exchanges are uncomfortably upfront about how they influence the price of their tokens. While exchange tokens seem to be taking the crypto market by storm, be aware that they are fundamentally tied to their parent exchanges. If Binance, Huobi or FTX were to experience significant issues or even shut down, then BNB, the Huobi token or FTT would all become worthless overnight. On the bright side, this dependence means there's no point in taking those tokens off exchanges for safekeeping. For all your other cryptocurrencies, remember the golden rule; "not your keys, not your crypto". Always keep your funds in your personal wallet when you're not trading.